Eメール時代の
グローバル ビジネス英語

Global Business English for E-mails and Letters

福田　靖　著

SEIBIDO

はしがき

　本書は、英語によるビジネスコミュニケーションスキルのうちの、主としてリーディングスキルとライティングスキルの基礎力向上のために書かれたものです。英語を母語としない日本人にとってのビジネス英語スキルはライティングの方がより重要であるという観点に立ち、グローバルビジネス社会の中で、仕事として通用する、きちんとした英語が書けるようになることを目指しています。

　ビジネス英語を自由に運用するためには、それが用いられるsituationが十分に分かっていなければならないので、ビジネスに関する知識、ビジネスの戦略・センスに基づいた英語力の向上が必要です。本書には、貿易取引を中心とするグローバルビジネスの現場で用いられるさまざまなEメールやレターのsampleを紹介していますので、ビジネス取引の実態と、ビジネス英語特有の用語や表現について学ぶことができます。また各chapterのsample mailで扱い切れない用語や、表現をexerciseの形で紹介しています。これらの表現の素材をうまく活用すれば、ビジネス英語の語彙や表現例、そしてbusiness writingのコツが身につくと思います。

　本書が学習者の、平易かつ実践でも使える、効果的な英文Eメールや英文レターを書く時の参考になることを願っています。本書の英文校閲を快く引き受けてくださったカリフォルニア大学（UCLA）のJudy Shane氏に心より感謝申し上げます。

2010年1月25日
著者

目　次

PART I	グローバルビジネスとコミュニケーション	4
CHAPTER 1	ビジネスコミュニケーションと英語	4
CHAPTER 2	レターとEメールのフォーマット	11
PART II	オフィスの英語	19
CHAPTER 3	電話の英語	19
CHAPTER 4	海外出張の英語	24
CHAPTER 5	ビジネス社交の英語	30
PART III	グローバル取引の英語	35
CHAPTER 6	取引申し込みの英語	35
CHAPTER 7	引合いの英語	42
CHAPTER 8	オファーの英語	47
CHAPTER 9	注文の英語	52
CHAPTER 10	契約書の英語	57
CHAPTER 11	信用状の英語	63
CHAPTER 12	出荷の英語	71
CHAPTER 13	決済の英語	77
CHAPTER 14	クレームの英語	82

PART I　　グローバルビジネスとコミュニケーション

Chapter 1　　ビジネスコミュニケーションと英語

ビジネスコミュニケーションの概念

　ビジネスの世界は急速に変化しています。一つはビジネスのグローバル化であり、もう一つはビジネス内容の多様化です。それに伴ってビジネスのやり方、コミュニケーションの仕方も大きく変容してきました。一口にビジネスコミュニケーションといいますが、【1-1図】に示すように、メッセージの内容、コミュニケーションの場、当事者、形式などによってさまざまなとらえ方があります。

ビジネス英語の考え方と特徴

　従来のグローバルビジネスコミュニケーションは電報、テレックス、レターを中心として行われていましたが、最近は、電話や、ファックス、それにインターネットのE-メールやインスタントメッセージが多く用いられるようになりました。Eメールには、英語や日本語のメッセージだけでなく、複雑な文書、書類であっても、安い料金で、迅速に、そして手軽に送ることができるだけでなく、記録を残すことができる、保存、編集することによって反復利用が可能であるなど多くの利点があります。ただその手軽さゆえに，Eメールを不注意に利用すれば、文法や、表現の誤り、配慮に欠けたメッセージなどコミュニケーション上の問題を引き起こしやすいので、よりよいEメールの書き方を学ぶ必要があります。

【1-1図】 ビジネスコミュニケーションの流れ

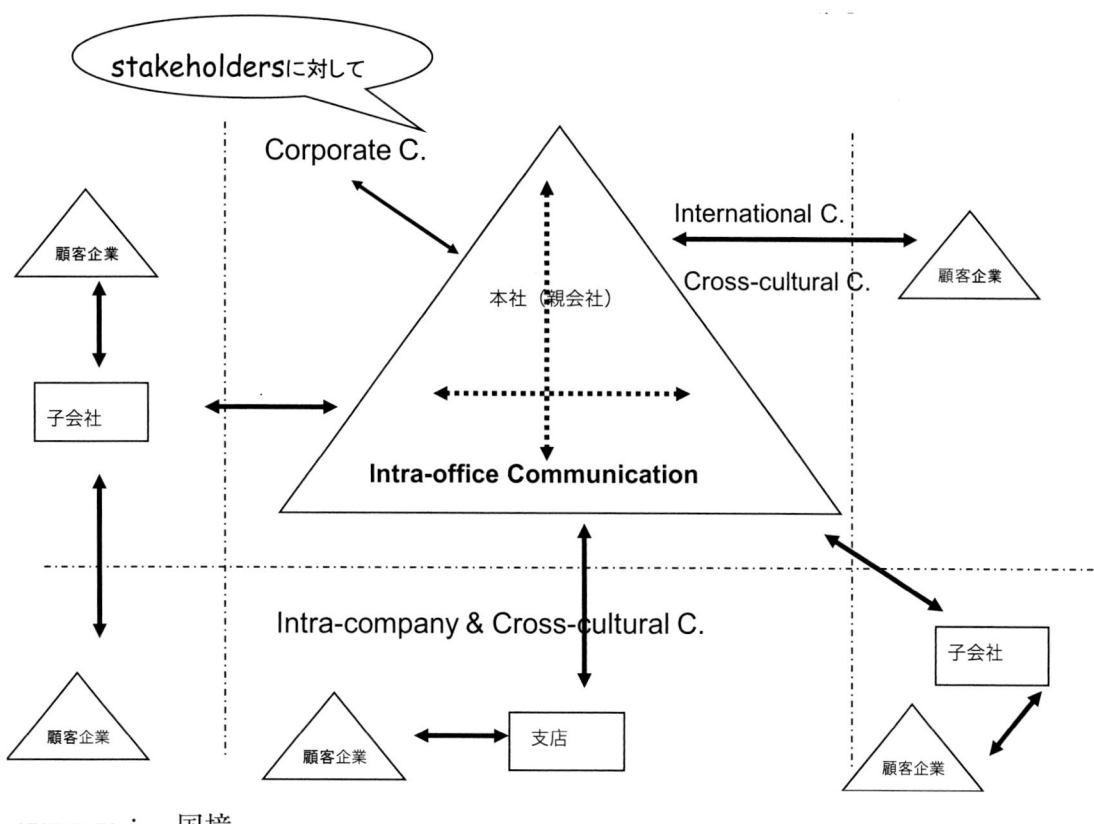

‒‒‒‒‒‒ ： 国境
⟵⟶ ： コミュニケーションの方向

　グローバルビジネスコミュニケーションにおいては、ビジネス英語が重要なツールになっています。と言っても、ビジネス英語という特別な英語があるわけではなく、それは語学力のレベルの問題ではないかとおもいます。基礎的な英語の能力を踏まえて、それがある程度レベルが高くなると、自然に話題の範囲も広くなり、オフィス内での雑談や社交の文書、業務の遂行などはすべてビジネス英語のレベルに達すると考えていいでしょう。結果的にはビジネスに関連のある用語やそれぞれのビジネスの分野で頻繁に用いる表現、あるいは英語を用いて書いたり、話したりするビジネス活動などを含めて一般にビジネス英語と呼んでいます。グローバルビジネスの世界では英語の使用が不可欠になっていますが、それも英米の国だけでなく、カナダやオーストラリア、それにヨーロッパやアジア諸国など非英語圏の国々でも、グローバルビジネスにおいては共通の言語としてはほとんど英語、すなわちビジネス英語が用いられます。

　それぞれの国の英語には語彙や、発音、表現に多少の差異がみられます。英語を母語(mother tongue)としない私たちは基本的に、アメリカ英語またはイギリス英語を学ぶ機

会が多く、それだけが正しい英語だと考える傾向がありますが、英語には地域や国によって多くのvariationがあり、多くの人々によってさまざまな英語が用いられ、それぞれの地域で定着しているということも知っておく必要があります。グローバルビジネスの世界では、世界の共通語として、多くのvariationをもったさまざまな英語が飛び交っているのでglobal Englishと呼んでもいいかもしれません。

　英語は、グローバルビジネスを円滑に遂行するコミュニケーションに必要な重要なツールです。同時に、コミュニケーションは、多くの場合、言語や文化を異にする人々の間で行われる(cross-cultural communication)のですから、誰にでも理解できる言葉でなければなりません。その目的にかなうものがglobal Englishと言えることになります。
　言いかえれば、ビジネスの実務においては、文学作品や学術雑誌のように、あまり難しい語やあいまいな表現、古めかしい表現は、難解であったり、誤解を招いたりするので好ましくありません。それよりも、誰にでもわかりやすい、いわゆるreadable Englishの方が望ましいわけです。
　現在イギリスやアメリカを中心に、Plain English Campaignという運動が広がっています。法律の条文や行政に関する文書を一般の人たちにも理解しやすいようにやさしい英語(plain English)で書きなおそうという動きですが、その基本的な考え方はビジネス英語についても当てはまります。
　しかしながら、いくら易しく、なじみのある表現が望ましいといっても、特定の地域だけの表現や、trendyな表現は異文化間コミュニケーションには適していません。例えばアメリカでは、会話の中ではwanna (want to), gonna (going to), ain't (am not/is not/was not/has not)などが頻繁に使われますし、以下のような表現や用語も、親しい同僚間の会話やe-mailなどではよく用いられる表現です。しかし、あまりに砕けすぎた表現は丁寧さに欠け、相手によっては失礼（impolite, rude）になるので、ビジネス、特に外国の顧客とのレターやe-mailでのコミュニケーションにおいては適しているとは言えません。

口語的すぎる表現	望ましい表現
I got a letter	I receive a letter.
Please ship this off the quickest way./ I need this there yesterday.	Please make the shipping as soon as possible.
Xerox 3 copies of this.	Could you make 3 copies of this?
We're all stocked up.	We have plenty of stocks now.
I wanna buy this. /Gimmy this.	We would like to order this item.
This is 5 bucks. Take it or leave it.	We offer this item at five dollars.
It's a piece of cake.	We are willing to change our terms.
You know what I'm saying?	You will kindly understand what I am explaining.

　国際ビジネスコミュニケーションで用いられる英語は、一般消費者を対象とするわけではなく、プロ同士がコミュニケーションをする時の英語でもあります。したがって、グローバルビジネスのための英語は、文化的背景を異にするビジネス人どうしで用いられる、わかりやすいplain Englishが望ましいと言えるわけです。ビジネスの専門家どうしで行われるコミュニケーションですから、特定の国や地域独特のくだけ過ぎる言い回し(colloquialism)よりも、貿易取引の専門用語(technical terms)や国際的に慣用的な表現を用いた方が誤解が少なく、かえってわかりやすいということもあります。

　Eメールやレターを書く場合も、常に相手(reader)に配慮し、簡潔であると同時にprofessional mannerにかなった、丁寧な表現(courteous expression)であることを心がけるべきです。

　具体的にplain Englishのいくつかの特徴をあげてみます。(巻末のCheat Sheet 1 も参考にしてください。)

1. 一般的には難解な語(long words)よりも誰にでも理解できる平易な語（short and simple words）が好まれます。
Enclosed you will find supplementary materials pursuant to the conversation we had this morning on technical papers. けさ電話でお話した技術書類に関する補足資料をお送りいたします。
⇒ As we discussed on the phone this morning, we are enclosing some additional materials on technical papers.

2. 陳腐で古めかしい表現(clichés/ trite expressions)よりは現代的な表現(modern usage)が好まれます。

I take great pleasure in inviting you to attend an important seminar on the state-of the-art technology of mobile phone.

⇒ We are pleased to invite you to our seminar, which is about state-of-the-art mobile phone.

3. 複雑な文(long or wordy sentence)よりも簡潔な文(short sentence)の方が望ましいと言えます。

In the meantime, please do not hesitate to call upon us if there is some other way in which we can be of assistance.

⇒ Please let us know if there is anything else we can do for you.

Exercises

Exercise A 次の用語の意味を簡単に説明しなさい。

1. business communication: _____
2. management communication: _____
3. corporate communication: _____
4. international communication: _____
5. cross-cultural communication: _____
6. inter-office communication: _____
7. horizontal communication: _____
8. vertical communication: _____
9. nonverbal communication: _____
10. informal communication: _____

Exercise B 次の各文をより平易な文に書き変えなさい。

1. Please favor us with a copy of the catalog together with price list of the product you have recently developed. (simple word を用いて)

2. As things stand now, we are interested in pursuing the matter helping you market here in China. (short sentenceを用いて)

3. We beg to advise that our products' prices are quoted in U.S. dollars. (modern expressionを用いて)

4. We are ready to offer a special discount. (concrete wordを用いて)

5. We would like to order on a regular basis. (unnecessary wordを省いて)

Exercise C 次の各文を平易でreadableな文に書き換える場合、正しい語順に並べ替えなさい。

1. We acknowledge receipt of esteemed favor dated the 10th inst.
   you /letter /thank /April/ your /10/ for/of/.

2. The aggregate of your belated payment amounts to $750.
   due/ are /payments/ past/ you/ your/ $750/ in/.

3. A favorable resolution of this matter would very much facilitate business activities between us.
   greatly/ matter/ solving/ deepen/ relationship/ our/ would /this/ business/ .

4. Please do not hesitate to approach me should you have occasion to be in Japan.
   an/ contact /you /me /please/ to /visit/ if/ have /Japan /opportunity/.

5. For the sake of promoting our sales, we are now giving you a special accommodation by granting the terms of D/A.
   we/ promote /our /terms/ will /D/A /allow/ to/ you/ sales/ ,/.

Exercise D 次の英文の日本語訳を書きなさい。

1. Thank you for your e-mail of August 3.

2. As soon as the goods are ready for shipment, I will contact you.

3. We usually choose your hotel chain when our employees travel on business.

4. Let me know the day and time that would be convenient for you.

5. Please feel free to contact me by e-mail if you have any questions.

Exercise E 次の状況・内容でEメールまたは英文レターのメッセージを書きなさい。

【状況】
取引先の副社長のMr. Ellenaが2週間後にあなたの会社を訪問することになっているので、先方の会社の担当者Ms. Louise Jonesに以下の3点を連絡しておきたい。
① 宿泊先は大阪のプリンストンホテルに11月5日～8日を予約している。
② 関西国際空港に出迎えに行きたいので到着時間をしらせてほしい。
③ 大阪滞在中の日程は現在計画中だが、時間があれば京都観光を案内したい。

Chapter 2　　レターとEメールのフォーマット

レターのフォーマット

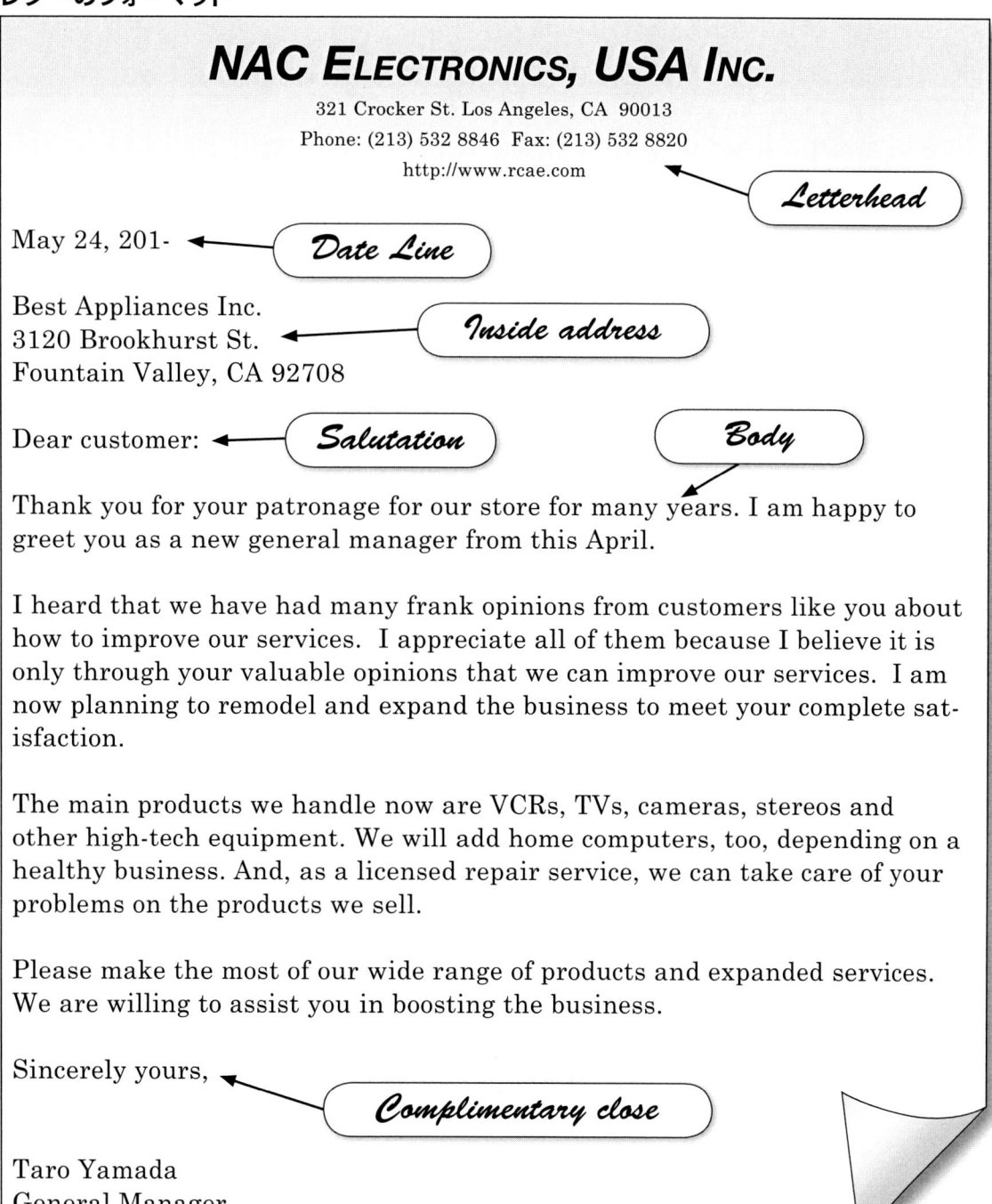

a licensed repair service = a service center licensed by the manufacturer
boost the business = increase the sales

Eメールのフォーマット

```
○○○                          E-mail
```

From: "Michael Jones" <mikejones@icbc.edu>
Date: 201-年 10月 23日 (月) 4:05 pm
To: fujita@jonan-gu.ac.jp   ← *Heading*
cc: jluisl@icbc.edu
Subject: Registration form attached

Dear Prof. Fujita,   ← *Salutation*   *Message* ↙

I am attaching a registration form, a conference brochure, and the tentative schedule of presentations.

There is accommodation available on campus at the cost mentioned in the registration form. However, if you would prefer to stay in a hotel, you may make your own arrangements.

Further information is available on our conference website – www.icbc/conf2015.com and the college website – www.icbc.edu.

I look forward to seeing you in Los Angeles.

Warm regards,   ← *Complimentary close*

===========================
Janice Freeman
Research Associate
R-23B, Communications Area
California College of Management   ← *Signature*
723 Wilshire Blvd.
Los Angeles, CA 90017
U.S.A
Tel: +1-312-4450 5546
E-mail: mjones@icbc.edu

(1) HEADING

1　FROMの部分には発信者名が入ります。企業間のコミュニケーションであっても、Eメールのアドレスは個人ごとに与えられているのが普通です。この例の場合、"Michael Jones"の部分は発信者名がわかるように登録したユーザー名で、それ以下がメールアドレスになります。メールアドレス（mikejones@icbc.edu）のうちmikejonesはユーザーのhandle名、@（at mark）以下はdomain nameと呼ばれています。domain nameは、企業、組織内でみな共通のものを使います。それは企業名やプロバイダーの名前(sony, ucla, nhk, aolなど)、組織の形態(.go, .org, .edu, .co, .ne, .com, .acなど)、そして国名(jp, us, ca, in, uk auなど)から成り立っています。

2　TOのところにはメールの宛先(受信者のメールアドレス)を入力します。

3　cc には、メールの同文を最初の宛先以外の人にも送りたいときにその人のメールアドレスを入れます。この場合、受信者は同文のメールがほかに誰に送られたかが分かるようになっています。

4　bccには、同文を最初の宛先以外の人にも送りたいが、その人に送っていることを宛先の人に知られたくないときにbccのあとに同文通知先のアドレスを書きます。

5　SUBJECT(件名)の後にはメールの内容がよくわかるような主題を書きます。レターでもsubjectを用いますが、Eメールの場合は、subjectがなかったり、あいまいだったり、不適切なものである場合は、spam mail/junk mailとして無視されたり、削除されることもあるので、受信者がメールを開く前に内容を推測しやすいようにできるだけ具体的な件名をつけるようにしましょう。

(2) MAIL TEXT

　　ここはメールのメッセージを書く領域ですが、メッセージはつぎの3つの部分から構成されるのが普通です。

　　6　　SALUTATION―冒頭挨拶(Dear Tom, Dear Mr. Walterなど)

　　7　　BODY ―メッセージの内容(本文)

　　8　　COMPLIMENTARY CLOSE ―結辞

　　　　　Formal:　　Sincerely yours, Sincerely,

　　　　　Informal:　 Best regards, Regards, Best wishes

　　　　　Personal:　 Thank you, Yours, Bye for nowなど

(3) SIGNATURE(発信者の氏名、部課、会社名、電話番号、メールアドレスなどの署名部分)

　　これらの構成要素はほとんどレターの場合と同じなので、レターとして書かれたものは基本的にそのままEメールとして送ることもできます。しかし、一般的に、Eメールはレターに比べてより簡略化され、informalな感じがします。

【Sample 1】

September 16, 201-
Dear Ms. Hirata,

Order Confirmation

Thank you for the order you placed on September 11, 201-. In all future correspondence regarding this order, please refer to order number 369141. Please review the details of your order below to make sure that it is accurate.

    Customer No.: 63631
    Shipping: USPS Priority Mail International (approx 9 days)
    Payment: VISA
    Billing and Shipping Address:
        Yumiko Hirata
        1-23-45 Akasaka
        Chuo-ku, Fukuoka 810-0015
        JAPAN

    Product: StarLife Glucosamine HCI 1500m/Cha 1200m
    Quantity: 5
    Price: $29.15
    Amount: $145.75
    Shipping & Handling: $43.54
    Total: $189.29

If you wish to make changes to your order, please contact Customer Service at (866)885-8622.
Thank you,

============================
Mary Jones
Shipping Department
BeautyCare.International, Inc.

    USPS=United States Postal Service
    Priority Mail International (PMI) is a means of sending correspondence and merchandise up to 70 pounds to over 190 countries and territories worldwide.

Exercises

Exercise A 次の略語の原語と日本語の意味を書きなさい。

1. c.c.   (   ) (   )
2. Ms.   (   ) (   )
3. Inc.   (   ) (   )
4. Co., Ltd.   (   ) (   )
5. Corp.   (   ) (   )
6. Ave.   (   ) (   )
7. Blvd.   (   ) (   )
8. CEO   (   ) (   )
9. e.g.   (   ) (   )
10. i.e.   (   ) (   )
11. ASAP   (   ) (   )
12. INFO   (   ) (   )
13. PLS   (   ) (   )
14. FYI   (   ) (   )
15. P. O. Box   (   ) (   )

Exercise B 空所の中から正しい語を一つ選びなさい。

1. I'll e-mail you in a couple of days to discuss the possibility of (having / doing / getting) business with you.

2. The recent rise in raw material costs has forced us to increase our prices by 5% (effective / affective / offensive) as from September 1.

3. (Check / Click / Pick) on www.greener.com to get our company profile.

4. If you have any questions, please e-mail me (to / in / at) the following address.

5. I'll call you early next week to discuss the trade fair, which will be (met / held / taken) in June in your city.

Exercise C 与えられた日本語の意味になるように空所に適切な語を記入しなさい。

1. 1月7日付レターありがとうございました。
   Thank you for your letter (　　　　) January 7.
2. 3月31日までにご承諾ください。
   Please let us have your acceptance (　　　　) March 31.
3. 29.49ドルの小切手をありがとうございました。
   Thank you for your check (　　　　) $29.49.
4. 今日の為替レートは1ドル101円です。
   Today's yen exchange rate is ¥101 (　　　　) the dollar.
5. 500台以上の注文には10%の値引きをいたします。
   We will be pleased to offer 10% discount for an order for 500 units (　　　　) more.

Exercise D 次の日本語を英語に直しなさい。

1. 出張　　　　(　　　　　　　　)
2. 名刺　　　　(　　　　　　　　)
3. 宿泊代　　　(　　　　　　　　)
4. 歓迎会　　　(　　　　　　　　)
5. 昼食会　　　(　　　　　　　　)
6. 創立記念日　(　　　　　　　　)
7. 旅行日程　　(　　　　　　　　)
8. 株主総会　　(　　　　　　　　)

Exercise E 次の内容で英文Eメールまたは英文レターのメッセージを作成しなさい。

【状況】
① 来週開催予定の支店長会議の案内確認(reminder)のEメールとする。
② 宛名は各支店長の山田氏、本田氏、Brown氏、Smith氏 (アドレスは適当に)
③ 念のために秘書の鈴木ひろみさんにも送る必要がある。
④ 控用に自分(総務課長下田一郎)宛てにも送っておくことにする。
⑤ 会議の主な内容は：今後の販売計画および新製品開発について
⑥ 日時：3月10日(水)午前10時より
⑦ 会場：本社第一会議室
⑧ 添付の資料を持参してほしい。

<BE一口メモ>

E-メールのnetiquette

最近のコミュニケーションの手段としてEメールはとても便利なものです。しかしあまり便利すぎるあまり、これを安易に利用すると思わぬ失敗をしたり、相手に失礼になったり、かえってコミュニケーションを損なうことにもなりかねません。Eメールの技術的な特徴および時差のある地域間での異文化コミュニケーションであるということを理解した上でうまくこれを利用することを心掛ける必要があります。

1. 緊急な場合（urgent or time-sensitive subjects）は電話でも連絡せよ。自分が送ったメールは必ずすぐに開かれるとは限らない。
2. 金銭、人事、個人情報などの秘密事項、重要事項の発表、複雑な問題、感情的な問題、怒りなどで興奮している時はメールは用いないほうがいい。電話、ファックス、直接面談などが有効。
3. E-メールははがきと同じ。掲示板に貼れないものは送るな（誹謗中傷、セックス、人種差別など）。
4. Spamとみなされやすい件名（salesのキャッチフレーズのようなもの）は避けよ。
5. フレーム(flame)メールやスパム（spam）メールは送らないようにする。
6. よほど正当な必要性がない限り多数の人にメールを送るな（spamと見なされやすい）。
7. メールはできるだけcc, bccではなく、正式の宛先欄アドレスをいれて直接送れ。
8. 不必要なメッセージを多数の相手にccで送るな(他人のアドレスを知らせることになる)。
9. スマイリー（emoticon）はビジネスでは用いないほうがいい。
10. 聞かれた質問にはすべて答えよ。さらに予想される質問にも答える情報を提供せよ。
11. 不要なファイル、大容量のファイル(memory-hungry attachment)は添付するな。
12. レターとは違う。長いメッセージは書くな。一つの文の長さは15～20語ぐらいが望ましい。（パソコン、携帯などのスクリーンは読みにくい）。
13. チェーンメールは転送するな（すべていたずらhoaxであるので、直ちに削除すべし）。
14. URGENT, IMPORTANTは使うな。ほんとに、ほんとに、ほんとに緊急な場合に使えなくなる（crying wolf）。
15. 誤送信を避けるため、また礼儀として、メッセージの最初には相手の名前（salutation）、最後には自分の名前(signature)を入れよ。
16. 返信の場合は、必要でない限り、相手からのメッセージを消し、件名を書き換えてから返信せよ。

PART II　オフィスの英語

Chapter 3　電話の英語

[Sample 2]

S: ABC Corporation. May I help you?
F: This is Mr. Clint Ford of American Trading Company.
S: Where can I direct your call, Mr. Ford?
F: Could I speak to Mr. Yoshida in the Export Department?
S: I'm afraid he is occupied at the moment.
F: Could you tell him I'll call again later?
　*　*　*　(later)　*　*　*
S: Mr. Yoshida, Mr. Ford of American Trading is on the line.
Y: Thank you. I'll take it in here.
　*　*　*　(later)　*　*　*
S: Mr. Ford, I'll put you through to Mr. Yoshida.
Y: Hello, Mr. Ford. How are you? I have been looking forward to your visit. Where are you calling from?
F: I'm staying here at Tokyo Grand Hotel. I'd like to see you on our new project. When are you available?
Y: I'll be completely tied up with visitors all day today. Would tomorrow morning be all right for you?
F: That'll be fine.
Y: Could you come to my office around 10 in the morning?
F: Sure. I will. Then, see you tomorrow.
Y: Thank you for calling.

[Sample 3]

S: Johnson Corporation. May I help you?

F: This is Hiroshi Tanaka with ABC Company, calling from Tokyo, Japan. Would you connect me with someone in charge of our company, please?

S: Wait a moment, Mr. Tanaka. Let me get you the person in charge.

C: Hello. Mr. Tanaka. This is Mark Chang. We are always satisfied with your service.

T: Hello. Mr. Chang. Thank you for your L/C No. 12345. We have just received it today.

C: I'm glad to hear that.

T: I'm calling today to discuss your order. We don't have enough goods in stock to fill your order.

C: I thought everything was on schedule. What's happened?

T: I am so sorry, Mr. Chang. We have had more orders than we expected, and the factory is temporarily unable to meet the demand.

C: What are the alternatives, then?

T: If you could wait till June, we could deliver your complete order. Or, we could ship half the order this week and the remainder in June. Which would be more convenient for you?

C: Well, our stock is running low, so could you ship half of it as soon as possible?

T: O.K. The first sailing opportunity would be "Shoei Maru," leaving Yokohama on April 16.
The ship is due in your port around April 22. I'll send you an e-mail when the shipment is finished.

C: O.K. I would like it as soon as possible.

T: One more thing I would ask you to change, Mr. Chang. Would you extend the expiry date of the L/C to the end of June to cover this split shipment?

C: Sure. I'll arrange for the amendment and get back to you as soon as the procedure is filled out.

T: We'll try to do our best to meet your satisfaction. Thank you for your understanding.

C: Thank you for calling.

Exercises

Exercise A 次の会話を聞いて空所に適当な語句を補充し、それぞれの役割で会話の練習をしなさい。

A: Hello, Phoenix Airlines, how can I provide you with excellent customer service today?

B: This is Izumi Berman and I would like to change the date of _____ on my upcoming trip to New York. I leave Wednesday.

A: I can make that change for you but there will be a fee of $100

B: That's fine but can you make sure I get an _____?

A: How does 10C sound? It is right near the front of the plane.

B: That _____. Thanks for your help.

Exercise B 次の英文の日本語訳を書きなさい。

1. Sorry. I didn't catch your name.

2. I'll put you through with Mr. Yamamoto.

3. Mr. Smith is not available right now.

4. Do you have a message for him?

5. Can I leave a message?

Exercise C 空所の中の正しい語を一つ選びなさい。

1. Will you (hold / put / take) on for a moment?

2. Thank you. I'll (keep / call / take) it in here.

3. I'll be in (touch / place / access) with you.

4. I'll (hold / give / leave) you a call tomorrow afternoon.

5. What time will you (get on / get to / get) here?

Exercise D 与えられた日本語の意味になるように空所に適切な語を記入しなさい。

1. 内線の4274番をおねがいします。
   (   ) 4274, please.
2. スミスさん、電話ですよ。
   Mr. Smith, someone is (   ) the phone for you.
3. ジョーンズさんと面会の約束をとりたいのですが。
   I'd like to (   ) an appointment to see Mr. Jones.
4. スミスさんいらっしゃいますか。
   May I speak (   ) Mr. Smith?
5. 伝言を承りましょうか。
   May I (   ) a message?

Exercise E 次の日本語を英文に直しなさい。

1. 彼と全く連絡が取れません。

2. お名前はどんなスペルでしょうか。

3. ジョーンズは1番で話し中です。

4. 後でかけ直します。

5. 来週は出張で留守をします。

Exercise F 次の内容で英文Eメールまたは英文レターのメッセージを作成しなさい。

【状況】
① 貴社が雑貨類を扱う一流の輸出商であることをインターネットで知った。
② 取引できるかどうか検討したい。
③ 営業案内および製品カタログを送ってもらいたい。
④ 当方の信用照会先として関西銀行大阪支店の名前を挙げることにする。

Chapter 4　海外出張の英語

[Sample 4]

E-mail

From:　"Nancy Smith"<nancys@rayl.com>

Date:　June 15, 201- 10:34 a.m.

To:　michikoh@totra.co.jp

Subject: Itinerary of Mr. Yoshida's U.S. Visit

Hi Michiko,
So that we can make sure that Mr. Yoshida's trip will be pleasurable, I have arranged his schedule according to his visiting period. He will:

August 10
- Arrive at Los Angeles International Airport on JL 62 at 11:00 a.m. local time on August 10 and depart for Las Vegas on American Airline Flight AA024 at 12:30 a.m.
- Arrive at Las Vegas Airport at 1:40 p.m. and check in hotel (Vellagio) at 4:00 p.m.

August 11
- Attend the Computer and Communication Exhibition (CCE) 201- , visit our booth, and meet customers
- Stay at the same hotel

August 12
- Depart Las Vegas Airport for Los Angeles on American Airline Flight AA035 at 10:10 a.m.
- Arrive at Los Angeles Airport at 11:20 a.m.
- Visit our office and meet president Rogers at 2:00 p.m.
- Go to our Lomita factory with Mr. Rogers and check in hotel (Long Beach Marriot) at 3:00 p.m.
- Meet with Mr. Williams, president of LGS Inc. and discuss new joint venture at the hotel at 5:00 p.m.
- Have dinner with Mr. Williams and Mr. Rogers after the meeting

August 13
- Leave Los Angeles for Narita on Japan Air Line Flight JL63 at 12:00 a.m.

Our staff members will be waiting for Mr. Yoshida at Transit Gate at Los Angeles Airport on August 10 and attend him to and from Las Vegas. I will send you the guidebook and map of Las Vegas soon. If he finds any interesting place, please let them know. They will be pleased to show him around the city. Please tell Mr. Yoshida that we all welcome his visit to our company.

With regards,
=============================
Nancy Smith
Overseas Sales Department
(310) 565 0717
"Nancy Smith"<nancys@rayl.com>

[Sample 5]

CONTINENTAL PARADISE HOTEL

15 Bencoolen Street, Singapore 189521
Phone: (65) 2337 0220, Fax: (65) 2337 1189
http://www.continentalhotel.com

July 26, 201-

Dear Guest,

<u>Technical Problem of Hot Water Supply System to Guestrooms</u>

Warmest greetings from Continental Paradise Hotel! I hope that you are enjoying your stay with us.

We would like to apologize that due to a technical problem in our hot water supply system yesterday, some of our guestrooms may have experienced a yellowish tinge in the hot water supply.

Our maintenance department did their best to amend the fault soon, and the system was operating as normal by 12 midnight.

We truly apologize again for the inconvenience this may have caused you, and thank you for your kind understanding and co-operation. If you have any questions, please feel free to contact me at Ext. 7085.

Sincerely yours,

Susan Chou (Ms)
General Manager

Exercises

Exercise A 次の会話を聞いて空所に適当な語句を補充し、それぞれの役割で会話の練習をしなさい。

A: Good morning, Mr. Suzuki. I've come to complete the contract with you for the business we've _____.

B: Well, we'll be glad to do so if you would accept our terms.

A: Yes, after careful consideration I've brought a draft contract with me. Would you like to go over it?

B: Mm. It looks good to me. So, I'll _____.

A: There is a copy for each of us. This one's yours.

B: I'm glad we were able to _____ an agreement. Our next job is to see that everything goes smoothly.

Exercise B 次の英文の日本語訳を書きなさい。

1. We are considering accepting some of your staff on a training workshop held at the head office here.

2. We would like to have your reply by the end of this week if possible.

3. I will be happy to attend the dedication of your new plant.

4. The main purpose of my visit will be to conclude our joint venture contract.

5. I just returned to work at the head office and am writing to say thank you for the hospitality you extended to me during my stay in Singapore.

Exercise C 空所の中の正しい語を一つ選びなさい。

1. Thank you for your e-mail (of / in / on) April 5.

2. I will send you our new catalog as soon as it comes (off / on / up) the press.

3. Please (convey / send / accept) my gratitude to your staff who showed us around your new plant.

4. I have a plan to go (on / to / for) a business trip to Europe in September.

5. After talking with my boss, I will (get / take / contact) back to you.

Exercise D 与えられた日本語の意味になるように空所に適切な語を記入しなさい。

1. お世話になりました同僚の皆さんによろしくお伝えください。
   Please give my best (　　　) to all of your colleagues I met there.

2. 早速のご返事ありがとうございます。
   Thank you for your quick (　　　).

3. ご訪問の手配をいたしますので、十分前もってお知らせください。
   Please let us know well (　　　) of time so that we can arrange for your visit plan here.

4. 東京にいらっしゃる間にお目にかかりたいですね。
   I will be pleased to (　　　) you when you are in Tokyo.

5. 10日の火曜日にもし1,2時間お時間があったらそちらにまいりますのでご都合のいい時間をおしえてください。
   If you are free for a couple of hours on Tuesday, the 10th, please suggest a (　　　) time and I'll be there.

Exercise E　次の文を英文に直しなさい。

1. 来月は貴国に出張する予定です。

2. 私の出張の際お目にかかれる可能性があるかどうか伺いたいのですが。

3. 7月に米国を訪問しますので日程を調整中です。(schedule)

4. 10月7日の午前10時43分に、JAL 231便にてロサンゼルスに到着します。(flight)

5. 貴社ご訪問の折はおもてなしをいただきお礼を申し上げます。(hospitality, extend)

Exercise F　次の内容で英文Eメールまたは英文レターのメッセージを作成しなさい。

【状況】

① 5月10日にカナダで開かれるTrade Fairに参加した後でロサンゼルスの貴社を訪問して帰る予定だった。

② 国内での重要な用件のために急きょ海外出張を取りやめざるを得なくなった。

③ せっかくのご招待をうけ訪問を楽しみにしていたが残念である。

<BE一口メモ>

E-メールの効果的な使い方

1. お互いに知らない同士の相手には bcc で送る。
2. 正しいスペル、文法、パンクチュエーションを（スペルチェッカーを利用せよ）。
3. E メールは個人のもの。メッセージもできるだけ個人宛のトーンで。自動返信は効果的でない。
4. 返信の際はオリジナルメッセージを残しておいたほうが親切な場合がある（相手が脈絡をつかみやすくなる）。
5. 長いメッセージは避けよ。短い文とレイアウトを用いよ。スペース行を入れよ（紙よりもスクリーンは読みにくい）。
6. トーンやスタイルはレターよりも informal でよいが、personal なものより注意深く、きちんとした文になるように書く。
7. template の自動返信が有用な場合がある（出張の留守メッセージ、会社の道案内、営業時間案内など）。
8. 発信したメールのコピーが自分宛てに届く（bcc で）ようにして発信記録を残すと便利。
9. 受信メールの中で重要なメールや添付書類などはプリントして保存するようにする。
10. 送信者氏名や件名の語句でメールを検索することができる。
11. Inbox は 1 日数回はチェックせよ。1 日の終わりにはすべてのメールを処理せよ。
12. 即日返信せよ（同日中、または 24 時間以内に）。出来ないときはあとで連絡すると返信せよ。
13. subject line(件名)にはメッセージを要約したもの、意味のある件名を書け。
14. 略語（FYI, ASAP, BTW など）はビジネスでは避けたほうがよい。
15. 転送や引用のメッセージは、必ず自分のメッセージの後に ＞（greater than symbol）をつけて示せ(必要な時だけ)。
16. 装飾文字は、相手のメールソフトでそれを読めることを確認できない限り用いないほうがいい。（相手によっては plain text しか読めない場合もある）rich text, HTML ファイルは読めない場合があるので注意すべし。

Chapter 5　　　ビジネス社交の英語

[Sample 6]

MEMO

From:　　Taro Suzuki, Manager of LCP Department
Date:　　Tuesday, February 2, 201-
To:　　　Ryu Kondo, Sales Representative
Subject: Organizational change

Hi, Ryu,

This is to inform you that there will be an organizational change in our LCP business.

On March 1, 201-, Mr. Peter Martin will take over my responsibilities in managing the LCP business in the United States. Therefore, all LCP issues must be reported to him. Here are his contact details:

　E-mail: martin@calent.com.
　Cell phone: 310-101-3324
　Office phone and fax number: 310-101-2506

I'll return to the head office and will be focusing on developing and expanding LCP markets in USA, Europe, Latin America, and Australia. I would like to thank you very much for your support during the time I have worked with you.

You will soon be receiving an official letter from the head office in Tokyo.

Best regards,

　　　LCP = liquid crystal panel

[Sample 7]

MORLIS DENSHI INDUSTRIES CO., LTD.

1-2-3 Fujimi, Chiyoda-ku, Tokyo 102-1150, Japan
Phone: +81-3-4523-2277, Fax: +81-3-4523-2154
URL: http://www.morlis.co.jp

June 20, 201-

American Motors Inc.
321 N. Michigan Ave
Chicago, IL 60611
U.S.A.

Attention: Mr. Miles Thomas, President

Dear Mr. Miles Thomas:

To meet the growing demand for ecological energy products, we opened a new plant on June 14 specializing in manufacturing fuel cells.

The new plant will be headed by Takashi Kurita, the former technical manager of the head office.
With this new expansion, we believe we will be able to make a valuable contribution to the ecological energy development in the automobile industry.

The plant's new address, phone, and website information are as follows:

    Morlis U.S.A. Inc.
    340 Camino de la Reina
    San Diego, CA 92107
    Phone: (219) 581 5400
    Fax: (219) 581 5233
    http://www.morlisus.com

We sincerely appreciate your continued support of our business.

Thank you,
Mitsuo Sasaki, President

Exercises

Exercise A 次の会話を聞いて空所に適当な語句を補充し、それぞれの役割で会話の練習をしなさい。

A: Hi Mr. Brewer, we met last week at the Optical Network Conference in San Ramon.

B: Yes, how have you been?

A: Good. As we discussed I'm calling to see if you want to _____ to talk further about our product line.

B: We talked _____ here and yes, there is some interest. How about next week?

A: I can do Tuesday morning if you are free.

B: 10AM would be great if you can _____.

A: Definitely, I will see you then next Tuesday at 10AM at your office in San Jose.

Exercise B 次の英文の日本語訳を書きなさい。

1. I am delighted to hear that you have been appointed as president of American Trading Corp. I wish you the best for a long and successful tenure of office.

2. With deep sorrow, we announce the death of our president, Mr. Saburo Kinoshita, on March 15.

3. Please convey our heartfelt sympathy to Mrs. Johnson and her family.

4. I will be in San Francisco during April 12–15, and I would like to have you join me for lunch during that time.

5. We request the pleasure of your company for dinner on Saturday, May 10 at 6:00 p.m.

Exercise C 空所の中の正しい語を一つ選びなさい。

1. I will (get / contact / touch) back to you soon.

2. I apologize for the delay (for / in / on) replying to your e-mail of May 9.

3. I am writing to say how much we (appreciate / thank / grateful) your co-operation in researching the feasibility of new business.

4. Please e-mail me any time if I can be (with / of / for) any service to you.

5. Due to conflicting schedules, I will be unable to (join / add / invite) you at the dinner in honor of Mr. Taylor.

Exercise D 与えられた日本語の意味になるように空所に適切な語を記入しなさい。

1. 社長にご選任なされました由心よりお祝い申し上げます。
   I would like to (　　) my hearty congratulations on your election to the office of president.

2. ウェスターンエレクトロニックス社を代表しまして、社長ご就任を慶賀申し上げますとともに、御社の末永いご繁栄お祈りいたします。
   On behalf of Western Electronics, Inc., we extend to you our congratulations (　　) your taking office as president and wish you the continuing success of your company.

3. 5月23日午後6時よりプラザホテルにおけるパーティにご招待申しあげます。
   We would (　　) to invite you to dinner at Plaza Hotel on May 23 at 6 p.m.

4. よいクリスマスと輝かしい新年をお迎えくださるようお祈り申しあげます。
   I (　　) you a Merry Christmas and a prosperous New Year.

5. 南カリフォルニア地域の売り上げ増大にともない、3月22日づけでロサンゼルスに支店を開設いたしました。
   With the growing volume of trade in Southern California area, we started business at new branch in Los Angeles (　　) of March 22.

Exercise E 次の文を英文に直しなさい。

1. 12月1日付で事務所を移転しますのでお知らせいたします。(move)

2. 2012年がご繁栄とご健康な年でありますようにお祈りいたします。(prosperous)

3. もしお役に立てることがあれば、遠慮なく次のアドレスにメールしてください。(of service)

4. 山田氏のご逝去に対し衷心よりお悔やみ申し上げます。(express condolences)

5. 鈴木一郎が支店長に任命されました。(branch manager)

Exercise F 次の内容で英文Eメールまたは英文レターのメッセージを作成しなさい。

【状況】以下の内容で招待状への返事を書きたい。

① 貴社の創立30周年記念式へのご招待に感謝する。

② 貴国への出張を計画中なので7月13日から3日間ホテルを予約してもらいたい。

③ 便名が分かり次第お知らせする。

| PART III | グローバル取引のメール |

Chapter 6　　取引申し込みの英語

[Sample 8]

TOKYO TRADING CORPORATION

6-2-3 Akasaka, Minato-ku Tokyo　107-0052 Japan
TEL: 03-3568-6055　FAX: 03-3568-6056
URL: http://www.totocor.com

May 17, 201-

BestFoods Mart, Inc.
605 N. Lamar Suite 350
Austin, TX　78703
U. S. A.

Dear Mr. Hitt:

I noticed your name in the business matching site of JETRO in which you are seeking a market opportunity in Japan. I am writing to express our keen desire to do business with you.

I have more than 10 years of business experience in the United States and learned that you are leading food manufacturers with an excellent business performance and enjoying a high reputation among health-conscious people because of the variety of quality food specializing in health and organic food. We are interested in establishing a licensing agreement with you to produce and distribute here in Japan a line of products bearing your prestigious brand name "BESTFOOD."

We, Tokyo Trading Corporation, are one of the world's largest general trading firms based in Tokyo with many affiliated companies. The lines of our business range from importing and exporting almost all products from and to all over the world markets, to international construction projects. We have manufacturing and distributing facilities throughout the country. Enclosed is our company profile which explains the scope of our business activities.

Like you Americans, the health-consciousness of Japanese consumers also has recently been getting higher. They tend to value "health" food such as health supplements and other organic foods. We trust that if the manufacturing technology improves and if more efficient marketing methods are developed, the demand for these products would be huge in this country. In this licensing, you would receive certain percent of the royalty fee. We believe that this venture would present tremendous business opportunities for both of us. If this proposal meets your interest please let us know. We would like to discuss the possibility of doing business with you.

For our credit standing, you may refer to the Bank of Hinode, Akasaka, Tokyo. To contact us, please e-mail me at goroizu@ttcor.co.jp.

Sincerely yours,

TOKYO TRADING CORPORATION

Goro Izumi
Manager of New Business Department

[Sample 9]

Dear Mr. Yokota:

Thank you for your letter of March 10, 201-. We are glad to learn that you wish to open an account with us in the line of men's and women's clothes.

As requested, we are enclosing our latest catalogs which explain a wide range of items we produce. If any of the items listed in the catalogs meets your interest, please let us have your specific inquiry. We will be pleased to send you our quotation.

In the meantime, would you please let us have the name of your bank to whom we can refer for your credit standing.

Sincerely yours,

NOTHERN CHINA INDUSTRIES, CO., LTD.

Lu Zeng
Manager of Overseas Division

Exercises

Exercise A 次の会話を聞いて空所に適当な語句を補充し、それぞれの役割で会話の練習をしなさい。

A: Hi, my name is John Smith from Oriental Technologies and I'm here to see Abe Washington. I have a 10 o'clock appointment.

B: I will let him know you're here. Would you mind _____ in please? Also, I'll need to see your ID.

A: Sure, _____ my driver's license.

B: Thanks, here is your badge. Please have a seat. Mr. Washington will be with you in a moment.

A: While I'm waiting can you tell me where the men's room is.

B: Down the hall to _____.

A: Much appreciated.

Exercise B 次の英文の日本語訳を書きなさい。

1. Before starting our actual business, we would like to hear more about the background of your company.

2. Please let me know by return e-mail a convenient time and date when we could discuss prospects of agency agreement directly on telephone.

3. We appreciate your proposal. But we have no plan now to establish any agent in Viet Num.

4. We have seen your advertisement in Better Life and wish to have your illustrated catalog and current price list for maple syrup.

5. You have been recommended to us by the Osaka Chamber of Commerce and Industry as a reliable importer of medical machinery in China.

Exercise C　空所の中の正しい語を一つ選びなさい。

1. If you need any (farther / further / some) information, please let us know.
2. We have (learned / known / listened) from the JETRO business matching site that you are a supplier of a wide range of plastic products.
3. We are looking for a (reasonable / reliable / feasible) importer of electronic products in EU countries.
4. We would like to (trade / sell / act) as your selling agent.
5. If you find any interest in the items listed in our general catalog, please let us (give / have / offer) your specific inquiry.

Exercise D　与えられた日本語の意味になるように空所に適切な語を記入しなさい。

1. ご提案いただいた取引きの可能性について上司と検討したうえで2週間以内にメールでご連絡いたします。
   We will contact you by e-mail within two weeks after(　　　　)the possibility of the proposed business with our top management.
2. 取扱製品の一部を載せたカタログを同封しました。
   (　　　　)is our catalog showing part of the vast range of the products we handle.
3. 当社の主な製品は野菜、魚介類、肉類の冷凍加工食品です。
   Our main (　　　　)are frozen processed food like vegetables, fish and meat.
4. 当社の信用状態に関しては大阪シティ銀行にお問い合わせください。
   For our credit standing, please (　　　　) to the City Bank of Osaka.
5. 昨年11月にロサンゼルスで開かれた工作機械展でお会いしたことを覚えておられるでしょう。
   You may recall that we met last November at the Machine Tool Fair (　　　　)in Los Angeles.

Exercise E 次の文を英文に直しなさい。

1. 当社は福岡にある老舗の家具メーカーです。

2. 貴社製品について詳しい情報をいただければ幸いです。

3. 提案させていただいたビジネスについてのご意見をいただければ幸いです。

4. 当社は20年以上にわたってアジア諸国から各種籐製椅子を輸入しております。

5. 当社は各種消費財の輸入会社で独自の販売網を持っています。

Exercise F 次の内容で英文Eメールまたはレターのメッセージを作成しなさい。

【状況】
① 当社製品に興味があるとのメールに感謝する。
② 当社は創業80年以上の磁器メーカーである。
③ 国内外に充実した販売網を持っている。
④ カタログを送る。またご入用の品を知らせてもらえれば見積もりを送る。

<BEーロメモ>

英語の中のラテン語

ラテン語は古代ローマ時代にはヨーロッパ全体で広く用いられていた言語ですが、現在は聖書や教会のお祈りに用いられることがあるほかは日常語としてはどこでも使われていません。しかし、ラテン語の影響は多くの国の言語に大きな影響をおよぼし、英語の語彙の中ではギリシャ語、フランス語に比べて圧倒的にラテン語を語源とするものが多いと言われています。そして現在でも法律、外交、学術、ビジネスの分野ではラテン語がそのままの形で用いられているものも少なくありません。ビジネス取引の中でも多くのラテン語を目にすることがあります。

ad hoc	【形】、【副】計画的、常設ではなく必要に応じてなされる an ad hoc committee
bona fide	【形】真実の、本物の real, true: bona fide holders
e. g.	exempli gratia たとえば = for example
et al.	【副】名前を挙げていないそれ以外の人たちを挙げる時用いる = and others
et cetera	【副】etc. その他のもの(人) = and so on
ex	【前】(商)買主が商品の輸送、支払いの責任を負う起点の前につける ex works, ex ship
i. e.	id est すなわち=that is
infra	【副】以下に、下に=below　infra-【接頭】infrastructure 下部構造
lb.	【名】重量のポンド libra(=pound)
n. b.	【間】nota bene よく注意せよ =note well
per	【前】～につき、～ごとに =for each, during each hour, etc. per share, per hour
per annum	=per year The economy grew at an average rate of 6% per annum.
per capita	【形】【副】一人当たりの、一人当たりで Israel's per-capita income is comparable to that of Spain.
per se	【副】それ自体は、(他のものと切り離して単独で考慮する時) Money, per se, is not usually why people change jobs.
pro-forma	【形】仮の、見積もりの pro-forma invoice
p. s.	post scriptum 追伸 =postscript
re	【前】ビジネスレターで用件の前につける =concerning　Re: your complaint of April 8.
versus	【前】対(二人または二つのチームが対抗している時) the Giants versus the Tigers
vice versa	【副】今述べた状況と逆のことも正しいと言える
viz	【副】videlicet すなわち、換言すると = namely, that is to say

Chapter 7　引合いの英語

[Sample 10]

```
件名:     Inquiry about Model FG-336H
差出人:   "Lim"<klim@ jtra.com.sg>
日付:     201-年10月16日(木)1:17 p.m.
宛先:     "Uchida"<suchida@tchem.co.jp>
```

Dear Mr. Uchida,

We are in the market for electronic toilet seats and are interested in your new model FG-336H.

We need to know if your products can fit the toilets commonly used in this country. Would you please send us the specifications for this model together with the CIF Singapore price on 500 sets?

We are waiting for your prompt reply.

Sincerely yours,

==========================
Kenneth Lim
Phone: 27 21 926 2340
Fax: 27 21 926 2346
e-mail: "Lim"<klim@ jtra.com.sg>

[Sample 11]

PCS Communications Inc.

445 Rodeo Street, Santa Monica, CA 90215, USA

June 8, 201-

Mr. Ichiro Matsui
Manager of Overseas Division
Kanto Electronics Co., Ltd.
4-12-25 Nishiazabu
Minato-ku, Tokyo 106-7525
Japan

Dear Mr. Matsui:

We are interested in your new DVD Player, Model RX-55T, which you advertised in the June issue of *Music Today*. We are writing with a keen desire to do business with you.

We have been leading importers of electronic products in this country for over 25 years. If you are interested in doing business with us, please let us have a copy of the catalog of the above model together with the lowest price CIF Los Angeles. For our credit standing, you may refer to the Bank of California, Santa Monica.

We are waiting for your favorable reply soon.

Sincerely yours,

Anna Clinton
Import Manager

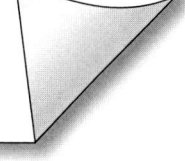

Exercises

Exercise A 次の会話を聞いて空所に適当な語句を補充し、それぞれの役割で会話の練習をしなさい。

A: Before we _____ this, I want to clarify some points.

B: Which ones?

A: When can we expect delivery? Is it possible for you to ship in August?

B: If you place your order with us within a week or so, we can ship the goods in August.

A: Another thing. Do you offer a discount for _____?

B: Well, we do discount, if your order _____ a minimum dollar amount.

Exercise B 次の英文の日本語訳を書きなさい。

1. We would ask you for a quote on the products on the attached list, giving your prices CIF Hakata, earliest delivery date, and terms of payment.

2. Will you please send us your catalog with the specifications of the new model RS25 together with CIF Yokohama price and other terms and conditions.

3. Could you please let us know by return e-mail the best price for VP-445T and delivery terms for quantities of 2000 sets.

4. Thank you for your interest in our product I/Nos.105 and 107. We are pleased to send you our quotation on CIF Pusan basis.

5. With this new branch, we will be able to provide our customers with better access and services.

Exercise C 空所の中の正しい語を一つ選びなさい。

1. We are in the market for stainless-steel kitchen utensils of Japanese (make / made / making).

2. Will you please send us a sample and a catalog of this (mode / model / make)?

3. We are attaching our (current / last / late) catalog. If there are any items you find of interest, please let us know. We will be pleased to give you a quote on them as soon as possible.

4. As requested, we have dispatched today five types of samples of coffee cups by air parcel. We hope they will arrive safely and (take / prove / meet) your approval.

5. If you need any (farther / further / longer) information, please let us know.

Exercise D 与えられた日本語の意味になるように空所に適切な語を記入しなさい。

1. この商品の神戸港本船渡し条件での最低値段を見積もってください。
   Please (　　　) us your lowest FOB Kobe prices for these goods.

2. 金額で5000ドルを超えるご注文には5％の割引をさせていただきます。
   We will be pleased to offer you a 5% discount on all orders (　　　) $5,000 in value.

3. 5月1日付e-メールでのご依頼により、最新のカタログとCIFシンガポール建ての価格表を添付いたします。
   As (　　　) in your e-mail of May 1, we are attaching our latest catalog together with a price list CIF Singapore.

4. 引合いをいただいた商品は現在在庫切れですので、出荷の準備ができましたら見積もりを差し上げます。
   The goods inquired (　　　) are out of stock now. We will send you our quote when we are ready for shipment of the goods

5. 当社製軍手の見本と価格をご依頼くださりありがとうございました。1週間お待ちいただけたらFOB ジャカルタの見積もりを作成し、見本は航空便でお送りします。
   Thank you for your request for samples and prices on our Work Gloves. Please allow us a week to prepare a quotation FOB Jakarta and send you the samples by (   ).

Exercise E　次の文を英文に直しなさい。

1. 当社は各種健康食品を扱っております。(handle)

2. 当社の新製品に対する2月10日付の引き合いありがとうございました。(inquiry)

3. この商品にはアジア諸国から多くの引き合いがきております。

4. 以下の商品を提供できるかどうかおしえてください。(supply)

5. 商品番号GR-22とGR-33はともに生産中止のために手に入りません。

Exercise F　次の内容で英文Eメールまたは英文レターのメッセージを作成しなさい。

【状況】
① スーツケースの引合いに感謝する。
② 見積もりとカタログを送る。
③ 当社の製品はデザインと色が豊富。
④ 在庫から提供できる。

Chapter 8　オファーの英語

[Sample 12]

White Bear Vineyards Inc.
1234 Solano Avenue, Napa, CA 94567 USA
Phone: 1-707-543-2500, Fax: 1-707-543-1230

April 4, 201-

Heisei Foods Co., Ltd.
2-3-25 Kibogaoka
Chigusa-ku, Nagoya 464-0015
Japan

Dear Sir/Madam:

Your name was suggested by the Business Opportunities site of JETRO on the Internet. We have learned from the site that you are looking for an exporter of Californian wine and we are writing you to express our keen desire to do business with you.

We put a new organic wine, developed through our unique biotechnology, on the market last year. Thanks to the growing demand for natural foods, our sales have increased by 40% this year in the overseas market. We believe that this kind of wine would meet Japanese tastes, too.

Enclosed are our company guide and recent product catalog. If you have any interest in doing business with us, please let us know the rough quantity required. We are ready to send you free samples and quote both FOB and CIF prices.

To contact us, please e-mail me at tomsmith@whitebear.com.

Sincerely yours,

Thomas Smith
Sales Manager

[Sample 13]

Nantong Sports Industry Co., Ltd.
Beijing, China

Dear Mr. Ryu,

Thank you for your e-mail of June 25 offering us 500 Fishing Rods, NP-F146E, at $95.00 per piece CFR Kobe.

To answer the offer, we very much regret to say that our customers here find your price too high and out of line in the prevailing market. Our information indicates that the similar types of fishing rods made in Korea are available at $55.00 per piece.

Unless we can present a more competitive price, it may not be possible for us to persuade our customers to accept your offer. We would ask you, therefore, to reduce your price by 10% at least.

In view of our long-standing business relationship, we would like to make you this counter-offer. As the market is declining, we hope you will consider our counter-offer most favorable and send us your acceptance by e-mail.

We are looking forward to your early reply.

Sincerely yours,
NAKAHARA FISHING INC.

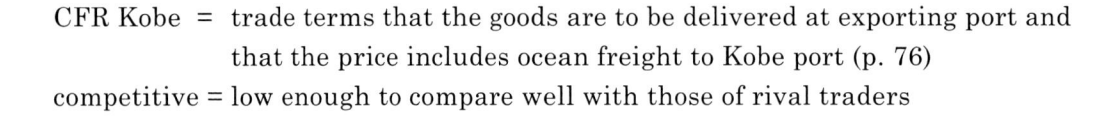

CFR Kobe = trade terms that the goods are to be delivered at exporting port and that the price includes ocean freight to Kobe port (p. 76)
competitive = low enough to compare well with those of rival traders

Exercises

Exercise A 次の会話を聞いて空所に適当な語句を補充し、それぞれの役割で会話の練習をしなさい。

A: Do you quote CIF or FOB?

B: All prices are FOB.

A: But, our preference would be for you to quote CIF Pusan.

B: We can do that. We'll work out our CIF quote tonight and _____ to you tomorrow morning. But could you give us a _____ idea of how much you're going to order?

A: I think it's better for you to quote your price first. The size of our order depends very much on your price.

B: All right. _____ what we can do.

Exercise B 次の英文の日本語訳を書きなさい。

1. Thank you for your inquiry. I will contact you as soon as possible.

2. To answer the inquiry, we are pleased to offer you 2,000 LCD panels for flat-screen television, SX-32, at $85 per sheet based on FOB Kobe.

3. Prices are based on FOB Nagoya, but we can also make up CIF prices and delivery at any port of your country.

4. The model you inquired about is out of production, but we can offer you a good substitute.

5. The price of raw materials has risen by more than 10 % due to the rise in oil prices, and we will have to increase our list prices.

Exercise C 空所の中の正しい語を一つ選びなさい。

1. We trust this offer will (prove / meet / fit) your satisfaction and immediate acceptance.

2. We offer you a 5% discount (for / off / from) our list prices.

3. We will keep this offer (open / correct / active) until September 30, 2009.

4. If your price is (cheap / competitive / inexpensive), we will be sending you a trial order.

5. As there is a great demand for these items, our stock has become very (little / small / low).

Exercise D 与えられた日本語の意味になるように空所に適切な語を記入しなさい。

1. 貴社の価格と同業者の価格には大きな開きがあります。
   There is a big difference between your price and (　　) of your competitors.

2. もしこの商品に興味がおありでしたらできるだけ早くご注文ください。
   If this offer interests you, please (　　) your order as soon as possible.

3. 下記の商品について最低価格を見積もってください。
   Would you (　　) your best prices for the items below?

4. 承諾のご返事が25日の火曜日までに必着することを条件として下記の商品をファームオファーします。
   We offer you firm the following product (　　) to your acceptance received here by Tuesday, the 25th.

5. 添付の価格表でご覧のように、すべての価格は大阪港本船渡し条件になっております。
   As you will see in the attached price list, all prices are (　　) on FOB Osaka.

Exercise E 次の文を英文に直しなさい。

1. この商品はきっと貴市場に適しているものと思います。

2. この商品は特にヨーロッパ市場では好評を博しています。(received favorably)

3. 代わりに、ご要求の品とほとんど変わらないS-225Hをオファーします。(identical)

4. これは当社取扱い商品のほんの一例です。(one sample)

5. このオファーは価格、納期ともに有利であることをきっとわかっていただけると思います。(advantageous/ useful)

Exercise F 次の内容で英文Eメールまたは英文レターのメッセージを作成しなさい。

【状況】
① 3月8日に当社のMR-22の値引きの依頼を受けた。
② ぎりぎりの価格でオファーしているのでこれ以上の値引きはできない。
③ 3月に発売されたばかりの新製品であり、注文が殺到していることを考慮してもらいたい。
④ 代替モデルとしてMR-11をお薦めする。品質はほとんど変わらず、価格は少し安い。
⑤ これは2年前のモデルであるので5%引きで提供できる。
⑥ どちらにするか3月25日までに返事してほしい。

Ten Tips for Business Writing

効果的なbusiness writingとは、依頼、通知、説得、拒絶などの目的を果たすことができるように、相手との関係に適したtoneで、状況を正しく反映したreadableなメッセージを伝えることが大切です。そのために役に立つヒント（tips）がいくつかあります。

1. 古い、陳腐な語句 trite phrases, cliches, and jargon) は避ける。
2. 長く、難解な語 (heavy words) よりも、短く、なじみのある語 (short, common and familiar words) を用いる。
3. 不要な語（unnecessary word）は省き、できるだけ短い文 (short, declarative sentences) にする。
4. 否定的な語 (negative writing) より肯定的 (positive words) な語、toneを用いる。
5. 受動態よりも能動態 (active voice) を用いる。
6. 項目が多いときはリスト（箇条書き）にする。
7. 項目を並べる時はパラレル構造にする。
8. 文の長さに変化を持たせる（1文のパラグラフも可能)。
9. できるだけ自然で、インフォーマルなスタイルで書く。
10. 文頭に And, Or, Because を置くことも可能。

Chapter 9　注文の英語

[Sample 14]

BUSINESS COMTEC CO., LTD.

5-23-11 Nishi-Nakajima, Yodogawa-ku, Osaka 532-0011, Japan
Phone: +81-6-2254-1200　Fax: +81-6-2275-1552

October 17, 201-

Mr. Clifford B. Johnson
American Business Machines, Inc.
W. 225 Exposition Street
Los Angeles, CA　90089-4351
U. S. A.

Dear Mr. Johnson:

Many thanks for your October 9 order that we received today for 100 units each of our Copying Machines, Model Nos. PS-55 and PS-66, which we offered you on September 25.

Unfortunately, PS-55 is temporarily out of stock, and it may take three months before we can ship the order.

If you need the products urgently, we suggest you increase the quantity of PS-66. Or, we will offer you a special discount of 3% on PS-55 if you are willing to wait for delivery.

We are waiting for your decision soon.

Sincerely yours,

Hiroshi Yamamoto
Overseas Manager

[Sample 15]

	E-mail
件名:	Order for DVD Player, XV-M2
差出人:	"Taro Tsukamoto"<tsukamot@bestcom.co.jp>
日付:	201-年10月23日3:47p.m.
宛先:	"Bui Quang Thao"<buiqt@luong.com>

Dear Mr. Thao:

Thank you for your catalog No. 12 for the DVD Player, XV-M2, together with your quotation.

The product meets our needs, and we wish to place the following order with you:

    Article: APPLE DVD Player, XV-M2
    Price: US$445.00 per unit, FOB Hai Phong
    Quantity: 200 units
    Shipment: during September
    Payment: 60 d/s, D/A

As the goods are consigned to Christmas and New Year sales, please note that we must receive them at the latest by the end of October to have sufficient time for unpacking and checking them before the sale.

We would appreciate your immediate and careful attention to this matter.

Sincerely yours,

===========================
Taro Tsukamoto
Import Manager
Best Communications Co., Ltd.

Exercises

Exercise A 次の会話を聞いて空所に適当な語句を補充し、それぞれの役割で会話の練習をしなさい。

A: Good afternoon, Mr. Brown! My name is Tanaka, with Kyowa Corporation, U.S.A. in Los Angeles. We are an importer and distributor of plastic polymers. It has come to my attention that you are in the plastic molding business. _____ right?

B: Yes, we do some injection molding here.

A: Well, if you don't mind, could you send me your product information by e-mail?

B: Sure, I will. _____ your e-mail address.

A: O. K. My e-mail address is t-a-n-a-k-a-@-k-y-o-w-a-.-com.

B: I've _____. Thank you, Ms. Tanaka. I'll e-mail you in an hour.

Exercise B 次の英文の日本語訳を書きなさい。

1. We are sorry we are unable to provide the quantity of your order within the date contracted.

2. We regret that we cannot place an order with you because your specifications do not meet our standards.

3. We will be unable to fill your order for at least two months because we are fully occupied with prior orders.

4. Please let us know the lead time from the receipt of order to the time of shipment.

5. We are sorry that we are unable to fill your order because the goods are out of stock now.

Exercise C 空所の中の正しい語を一つ選びなさい。

1. If your quality (comes / puts / meets) up to our standards, we will place our regular orders with you in the future.

2. You may be assured that we will do our best to (carry / place / execute) your order in a satisfactory manner.

3. If your prices and terms are satisfactory, we will (send / comply / place) our first order with you.

4. Please note that the goods will be (entered / covered / paid) by us in this country.

5. The goods are urgently (needed / sold / stocked); we hope you will speed up your shipment.

Exercise D 与えられた日本語の意味になるように空所に適切な語を記入しなさい。

1. 日本製ゲーム機の購入に関心がある顧客は少なくありません。
   We have many customers who are very interested in buying the video game machines of Japanese (　　　).

2. もしこの注文の調達に満足できれば大量に追加注文します。
   If this order is carried out satisfactorily, we will (　　　) an order on a large scale.

3. 貴社の見積書に載っている全商品を注文することに決定しました。
   We have now decided to place an order (　　　) you for all the items in your quotation.

4. もし品質が見本通りであれば、大量に注文します。
   If your quality is (　　　) to that of the sample, you may expect a sizable order.

5. 貴社の仕様が当社の基準に合わないのでこの注文は取消します。
   We are writing to inform you that since your specifications do not (　　　) our standards, we will have to cancel our order.

Exercise E 次の文を英文に直しなさい。

1. もし品質に満足できれば大量注文します。(prove)

2. 4月15日付けの見積もりにより当社の注文117号を添付します。(quotation)

3. 一両日中にファックスで正式の注文書をお送りします。(formal)

4. ポータブルメモリープレイヤーR－V22を200台という注文書405号をありがとうございました。(portable memory player)

5. 追加注文がいただけることを願っています。(place)

Exercise F 次の内容で英文Eメールまたは英文レターのメッセージを作成しなさい。

【状況】
① 当地で開かれたトレードフェアで展示品を見学し商品カタログをもらった。
② 検討したら当社の基準に合うことがわかった。
③ RX-225型を8台、RX-226型を6台、RX-227型を6台試験注文したい。
④ ただし、当社の方針である一覧後30日払いのD/A手形での支払を条件とする。
⑤ こちらの信用状態はカリフォルニアユニオン銀行のロングビーチ(Long Beach)支店に問い合わせてほしい。

Chapter 10 契約書の英語

[Sample 16]

SALES CONFIRMATION No. SC-1234

Shanghai Fashion Co., Ltd. as Seller, confirm having sold to you as Buyer, the following goods by contract of sale made on the under date and on terms and conditions as specified below:

COMMODITY:	Cotton Tote Bag
QUALITY:	Sample Nos. 25B, 25W and 25G
QUANTITY:	30,000 pcs. (10,000 pcs. for each color)
PRICE :	US$8.50 per pc. CIF Kobe
TOTAL AMOUNT:	US$255,000.00
PACKING:	60 Carton Boxes (each containing 500 pcs.)
MARKING:	UNIC
	Kobe
TIME OF SHIPMENT	During October, 201-
PORT OF SHIPMENT:	Shanghai, China
PORT OF DISTINATION:	Kobe, Japan
PAYMENT:	Draft at sight under irrevocable L/C
INSURANCE:	All Risks, for full invoice amount plus 10%

Refer to General Terms and Conditions on the attached sheets, which are incorporated in and make a part of this contract.

Accepted and confirmed by

UNIC JAPAN CORPORATION	SHANGHAI FASHION CO., LTD.
by (*Buyer*)	by (*Seller*)
on September 5, 201-	on August 29, 201-

Please sign and return one copy.

at sight= of a bill of exchange, payable when presented to the debtor

[Sample 17]

AGREEMENT ON GENERAL TERMS AND CONDITIONS OF BUSINESS
The sale specified on the face is subject to the following terms and conditions.

1. Business: Business is transacted between Principals: both parties act on their own account and responsibility.
2. Price: Unless otherwise specified in e-mails, faxes or letters, all prices submitted by Seller or Buyer are on CIF Long Beach in US Dollars.
3. Order: All orders by telephone must be confirmed by writing on receipt. Orders confirmed in this way must not be cancelled without mutual consent.
4. Shipment: Seller must ship all the goods in good order. Unless otherwise specified on the face of this contract, partial shipment and transshipment are permitted. The date of bill of lading is taken as the conclusive proof of the date of shipment.
5. Force Majeure: Seller takes no responsibility for the delay in shipment due directly or indirectly to force majeure including fires, floods, earthquakes mobilization, war, civil commotions, prohibition of export, requisition of vessels, strikes, riots, blockade, and any other contingencies which prevent shipment within the period agreed upon.
6. Delayed Shipment: If shipment is prevented or delayed, in whole or in part, by the reason of force majeure, the period of shipment stipulated is extended for twenty-one (21) days. If shipment within the extended period is still prevented by the duration of the above mentioned causes or the result of any of them, it is at Buyer's option either to allow the late shipment of the goods or to cancel the order by notice in writing.
7. Payment: Seller draws at sight under irrevocable letter of credit for the full invoice amount. Buyer must open letter of credit for Seller immediately upon the conclusion of the contract.
8. Claims: Any claim by Buyer regarding the goods shipped must be notified in writing by Buyer to Seller within fourteen (14) days after arrival of the goods at destination. The certificates recognized by surveyors must be sent by mail soon.
9. Arbitration: Both parties must try to settle any dispute or claim arising out of this contract as amicably as possible. But when in failure, it is settled by arbitration in Japan, according to the Commercial Arbitration Rules of the Japan Commercial Arbitration Association. The award given by the arbitrators is final and it binds both parties concerned.

IN WITNESS OF IT, the parties have caused this agreement in English and duplicate to be signed by their duly authorized representatives.

	XYZ CORPORATION		ABC CO., LTD.
by	*(Buyer)*	by	*(Seller)*
on	February 8, 201-	on	February 1, 201-

principal= a person who authorizes another person to be his agent
force majeure= (F. super force) a cause or event which neither party to a contract can control such as action by a government in time of war, or strikes, and Act of God

Exercises

Exercise A 次の会話を聞いて空所に適当な語句を補充し、それぞれの役割で会話の練習をしなさい。

A: I am interested in _____ a large quantity of this material.

B: The price is $20 per square foot.

A: That's a bit expensive. What if I purchase 100 square feet, can you give me a discount?

B: I'd have to get my manager's approval but I think I can manage a 5% discount. So _____ be $1900.

A: Still too much. Is there anything else you can do?

B: If you are willing to pay in cash and purchase the material today I can make it $1800, including tax and delivery.

A: You have _____.

Exercise B 次の英文の日本語訳を書きなさい。

1. This agreement is made on July 4, 2015 between Nippon Trading Co., Ltd., called the "Seller," and American Corporation, called the "Buyer."

2. If the Buyer fails to open the letter of credit in time, the Seller has the right to cancel, without further notice, the whole or any part of this Contract and lodge a claim with the Buyer for losses sustained.

3. The Buyer must pay the total invoice amount to the Seller within thirty (30) days after the date of Bill of Lading by TT remittance to the following bank account of the Seller:

4. All disputes or controversies or differences which may arise between the parties out of or in relation to, or in connection to the breach of the contract, will finally be settled by arbitration in Tokyo.

5. If any discrepancy occurs between the terms and conditions of this Agreement and the written part of any Individual Contract, those of the Individual Contract prevails.

Exercise C 空所の中の正しい語を一つ選びなさい。

1. This Agreement is (rendered / closed / entered) into this first day of April, 2015 by Japanese Trading Co., Ltd. and Indian Corporation, Inc.

2. This agreement is (governed / made / consisted) by the laws of Japan without regard to the conflicts of law rules to it.

3. Please note that this contract can be extended another one year unless any (objection / obligation / suggestion) is offered by either party with one month's notice.

4. The Seller must warrants to the Buyer and to its customers that all shipments(uniform / conform / perform) to the samples and specifications.

5. We would appreciate your sending one copy of the contract back to us with your (signature / agreement / duplicate) on it.

Exercise D 与えられた日本語の意味になるように空所に適切な語を記入しなさい。

1. 契約は一方的に取り消すことはできない。
   Contracts cannot be cancelled (   ).

2. 売買確認書の原本を2部お送りします。
   We are sending you two (   ) of our sales confirmation.

3. 売主は、不可抗力的事故の場合は商品の全てまたは一部の不積みまたは船積み遅延に対しては責任を負わないものとする。
   The Seller will not be held (   ) for failure or delay in delivery of the entire lot or a portion of the goods in case of any Force Majeure accident.

4. 買主は発行する信用状の中に本契約書番号を引用するものとする。
   The Buyer must quote the number of this Contract in the letter of credit to be (   ).

5. 売主は買主に対して、当該製品が第三者の特許権、著作権、その他の知的財産権の侵害とならないことを保証するものとする。
The Seller warrants to the Buyer that the Products are (　　　　) from infringement of any patent, copyright or other intellectual property of any third party.

Exercise E　次の文を英文に直しなさい。

1. 取引は本人同士で行われるものとし、双方は自らの勘定と責任で行動するものとする。

2. 他に特に定めない限り、本契約のもとでは全ての見積もり及び価格は米ドルにてFOB日本港建てで行われるものとする。

3. 売買契約書を2部お送りしますので、ご署名の上1部をご返送ください。

4. 船荷証券の日付が船積日の決定的な証拠とみなさる。

5. クレームにはすべて売主が認める鑑定人承認の鑑定報告書を添付しなければならない。

Exercise F　次の内容で英文Eメールまたは英文レターのメッセージを作成しなさい。

【状況】
① 6月10日にデジカメS-50Vに注文をもらった。
② 同機種は在庫が切れており、先月生産中止になったのでもはや入手の見込みがない。
③ 代わりにS-50VEを薦める。
④ これは少し高いが品質は優れている。
⑤ 今なら市場開拓のために5%の割引で提供できる。
⑥ 6月30日までに回答してほしい。

<BE一口メモ>

英語の丁寧表現

　日本語の敬語体系は複雑で、日常会話だけでなく、ビジネスにおける書き言葉の中でも敬語をうまく使い分けることがコミュニケーションを円滑に進めるカギとなります。一口に敬語と言っても、お買い求めになる、おっしゃる、くださる、お越しになる、いらっしゃるなどの尊敬語や、差し上げる、申し上げる、承る、参る、存じ上げる、頂戴する、…いたすなどの謙譲語、そして送ります、ご注文、お問い合わせ、ご返事、…します、…です、…でございますなどの丁寧語もあります。このような敬語を正しく用いると、お互いの上下関係、親密度の違いに適したいろいろな表現ができます。英語には please, thank, appreciate, sorry などを除いて、日本語のように語彙そのものに敬語があるわけではありません。しかし語の組み合わせ具合によって丁寧さ、尊敬の表現をすることは可能です。したがって英語のコミュニケーションにおいては、文体の違いによる丁寧表現を覚えることが大切だと言えるでしょう。

1. Send me a sample.
2. Send me a sample, please.
3. Can you send me a sample?
4. Can I have a sample?
5. May I have a sample?
6. Could you send me a sample?
7. Could I have a sample?
8. Is it possible to have a sample?
9. I will be grateful if you will send me a sample.
10. I would be grateful if you could send me a sample.
11. If you don't mind, please send me a sample.
12. Would you mind sending me a sample?
13. Would you be so kind that I could have a sample?

Chapter 11　信用状の英語

[Sample 18]

E-mail

件名:　　Please open LC for Order No. 1125
差出人:　"Jack Bailey"<jbailey@pacificfood.com>
日付:　　October 19, 201- 2:13 p.m.
宛先:　　"Kojima Yukio"<kojima@sappari.co.jp

Dear Mr. Kojima,

This is about your Order No. 1125 of September 27 for 300 cartons of canned beer, "Zero Green."

I e-mailed you on October 5 inquiring when you would open your L/C and I received your reply saying that you would open it in a day or two. However, two weeks have passed, and I have not heard from you.

Please tell me what the situation is and please open the L/C soon to execute your order as agreed.

Best regards,
Jack
========================
Export Division
General Pepco Company Inc.
"Jack Bailey"<jbailey@pacificfood.com>

---

　　execute = to carry out; put into effect: *execute* a plan/order/contract

[Sample 19]

```
                              E-mail
件名:      L/C for Order No. 60 arranged
差出人:    "Jiro Yamada"<yamada@osakatra.co.jp>
日付:      July 15, 201-4:28 a.m.
宛先:      "John Ford"<johnf@taipeitra.com>
```

Dear Mr. Ford,

Thank you for your July 9 e-mail, confirming our Order No. 60.

I have arranged today for an irrevocable letter of credit for US$45,225 in your favor with the Kansai Bank, Osaka, as contracted.

Please let us know when you receive the credit and when the shipment is completed.

Best regards,

Jiro Yamada
Import Manager

    irrevocable = unchangeable/ final
    in your favor = to your advantage/ addressed to you

[Sample 20]

KOBE USJ BANK CORPORATION, SANNOMIYA,
7-6-54 GOKO-DORI, CHUO-KU, KOBE 650-0051

DATE: February 16, 201-
OUR ADVICE NO. 1234567

ADVICE OF IRREVOCABLE LETTER OF CREDIT

BENEFICIARY   Messrs. JAPAN MACHINERY TRADING CO., LTD.
                    4-3-21 KANO-CHO, CHUO-KU, KOBE 650-0050 JAPAN
                      FAX: 78-361-7200
                      TEL: 78-361-7311

ISSUING BANK   THE UNION BANK OF CALIFORNIA, TORRANCE
                    4567 LOMITA BOULEVARD, TORRANCE CA 90513 U.S.A.
                    SWIFT – MT700
                            L/C NO.: D321-L6543J
                            L/C AMOUNT: USD250,000.00

WE HAVE PLEASURE IN ADVISING YOU THAT WE HAVE RECEIVED
A CABLE DATED FEB. 16, 201- FROM THE ABOVE-MENTIONED BANK
REGARDING THE ISSUANCE OF THE CAPTIONED CREDIT AS PER
ATTACHED COPY.

ALL DRAFTS NEGOTIATED UNDER THIS ADVICE ARE TO BE ACOMPANIED
BY THIS LETTER, AND THE AMOUNT OF THE DRAFTS MUST BE ENDORSED
ON THE REVERSE HEREOF BY THE NEGOTIATIONG BANK.
Instructions * * (Please be guided by the following marked "X")
☒ We strongly recommend that the L/C should be carefully checked against the export contract to prevent possible problems.
☒ Unless otherwise expressly stipulated in the Credit, this credit is subject to Uniform Customs and Practice for Documentary Credits (2006) Revision) International Chamber of Commerce, Publication No. 600.
☒ We are unable to accept any responsibility for errors and/or omissions in the transmission or translation of the cable, or for any amendment which may be necessary upon receipt of the mail advice of this credit.
☒ Please note that this is merely an advice on our part.

ADVISING BANK:
KOBE USJ BANK CORPORATION, SANNOMIYA,
7-6-54 GOKO-DORI, CHUO-KU, KOBE 650-0051 JAPAN

27	SEQUNCE OF TOTAL			
	1/1			
40A	FORM OF DOCUMENTARY CREDIT			
	IRREVOCABLE			
20	DOCUMENTARY CREDIT NO			
	D321-L6543J			
31C	DATE OF ISSUE			
	FEBRUARY 14, 201-			
40E	APPLICABLE RULES			
	UCP LATEST VERSION			
31D	DATE AND PLACE OF EXPIRY			
	APRIL 20, 201-, JAPAN			
50	APPLICANT			
	REFER TO ITEM 1 UNDER SWIFT FIELD 47A			
41D	AVAILABLE WITH ... BY			
	ANY BANK			
	BY NEGOTIATION			
42C	DRAFTS AT			
	SIGHT IN DUPLICATE FOR 100PCT OF INVOICE VALUE.			
42A	DRAWEE			
	THE UNION BANK OF CALIFORNIA, TORRANCE			
	4567 LOMITA BOULVARD, TORRANCE CA 90513 U.S.A.			
43P	PARTIAL SHIPMENTS			
	PROHIBITED			
43T	TRANSHIPMENT			
	PERMITTED			
44E	PORT OF LOADING / AIRPORT OF DEPARTURE			
	KOBE			
44F	PORT OF DISCHARGE / AIRPORT OF DESTINATION			
	LOS ANGELES			
45A	DESCRIPTION OF GOODS			
	DESCRIPTION	QUANTITY (UNIT)	UNIT PRICE (USD/UNIT)	AMOUNT (USD)
	TERARA BORING			
	MILL T27	20	12,500.00	250,000.00
	+ TOTAL:	20 UNITS		USD250,000.00

	+ TRADE TERMS: CIF, LOS ANGELES
	+ PACKING: STANDARD EXPORT PACKING.
	+ ORIGIN : JAPAN
46A	DOCUMENTS REQUIRED

         + TRADE TERMS: CIF, LOS ANGELES
         + PACKING: STANDARD EXPORT PACKING.
         + ORIGIN : JAPAN

46A   DOCUMENTS REQUIRED
         1/ DULY SIGNED COMMERCIAL INVOICE 03 ORIGINALS
         2/ FULL SET OF CLEAN SHIPPED ON BOARD OCEAN BILLS OF LADING MADE OUT TO ORDER MARKED 'FREIGHT PREPAID' AND NOTIFIED THE APPLICANT MENTIONING FULL ADDRESS, TEL NO. AND FAX NO.
         3/ DULY SIGNED DETAILED PACKING LIST IN 03 ORIGINALS.
         4/ CERTIFICATE OF ORIGIN ISSUED BY AN AUTHORIZED AUTHORITY OF JAPAN IN 01 ORIGINAL AND 01 COPY.

47A   ADDITIONAL CONDITIONS
         1/ APPLICANT'S NAME AND ADDRESS: CALTEC CORP., 1234 CARSON BOULVARD TORRANCE, CA 90513 U. S. A.
         2/ ALL DOCUMENTS FOR NEGOTIATION MUST BE PRESENTED IN TRIPLICATE (UNLESS OTHERWISE STATED) AND QUOTED OUR CREDIT NUMBER.
         3/ SHIPMENT IS NOT LATER THAN MARCH 31, 201-.
         4/ ALL CORRECTIONS OR ALTERATIONS ON DOCUMENTS MUST APPEAR TO BE VERIFIED BY THE PARTY WHO ISSUED DOCUMENTS.

71B   CHARGES
         ALL BANKING CHARGES OUTSIDE THE UNITED USTATES, REIMBURSEMENT CHARGES, AMENDMENT CHARGES, DISCOUNT CHARGES AT BENEFICIARY'S A/C.

48   PERIOD FOR PRESENTATION
         WITHIN 15 DAYS AFTER SHIPMENT DATE BUT WITHIN L/C VALIDITY.

78   INSTRUCTIONS TO PAYING/ACCEPTING/NEGOTIATING BANK
         PLEASE SEND ALL DOCUMENTS IN COMPLIANCE WITH ALL TERMS AND CONDITIONS OF THE CREDIT TO THE UNION BANK OF CALIFORNIA, TORRANCE BY DHL SERVICE ON NEGOTIATING DATE IN ONE LOT.

KOBE USJ BANK CORPORATION, SANNOMIYA,

....
AUTHORIZED SIGNATURE

Exercises

Exercise A 次の会話を聞いて空所に適当な語句を補充し、それぞれの役割で会話の練習をしなさい。

A : When can you ship the sample to us?

B : _____ from the factory that it will take about one more week.

A : _____ ask your factory to expedite the shipment?

B : Yes, I will follow-up with them again.

A : The sooner the better. We _____ right away.

B : OK. We will do our best.

Exercise B 次の英文の日本語訳を書きなさい。

1. Will you please open the covering L/C in time to secure early shipment.

2. Please note that your L/C must reach us 20 days before shipment.

3. Please do not insert any clause that is not agreed upon in the contract.

4. Please open an L/C as soon as possible so that we can execute the order smoothly.

5. Will you please extend the shipment date of your L/C to June 10 and validity to June 30.

Exercise C　空所の中の正しい語を一つ選びなさい。

1. As this is your initial order, we would appreciate your arranging for an irrevocable letter of credit in our (favor / address / benefit).

2. L/C No. T2345 to cover your Order No. 50 (offered / effected/ issued) by the Bank of America has arrived today.

3. We would ask you to amend the L/C (opening / extending /putting) the expiry date to August 15.

4. Other(terms / validity / amendment) and conditions of the credit remain unchanged.

5. We have not yet received an L/C to (effect / pay / cover) your Order No. 250.

Exercise D　与えられた日本語の意味になるように空所に適切な語を記入しなさい。

1. 貴社を受益者として当該信用状を開設するよう香港第一銀行に手配しました。
   We have arranged with the Hong Kong First Bank to (　　) the covering L/C in your favor.

2. 1週間前にEメールを差し上げましたが、この件に関して何らお知らせをいただいていないようです。
   I sent you my e-mail a week ago but apparently I have not received any further news (　　) this matter.

3. ご注文205号をカバーする信用状を開設していただくよう再三お願いをしましたが、まだ届いておりません。
   We have requested repeatedly that you open an L/C (　　) your Order No.205, but we have not received it yet.

4. 貴信用状を受領後2週間以内に出荷できます。
   We can ship the goods within two weeks after (　　) of your L/C.

5. 商品は船積みの準備ができておりますので、当該信用状の手配をお願いします。
   The goods are ready for shipment. Please arrange (　　) the covering L/C.

Exercise E 次の文を英文に直しなさい。

1. 通常は新規の顧客には取り消し不能信用状による支払いをお願いする方針になっております。(irrevocable letter of credit)

2. 10月10日までに信用状が届かなければ、契約期日までに船積みできません。(only if)

3. 信用状がなければ手形を買い取ってもらえないことをご了承ください。(negotiate draft)

4. 信用状の総額は15,700ドルではなく、17,500ドルでなければなりません。(read, instead of)

5. 信用状の期限を11月末日まで延長してください。(expiry date)

Exercise F 次の内容で英文Eメールまたは英文レターのメッセージを作成しなさい。

【状況】
① ご注文25号は契約通りに出荷できるはずだった。
② 工場ストのために出荷予定日に間に合いそうにない。
③ 信用状の船積み日を9月15日まで延ばしていただきたい。

Chapter 12   出荷の英語

[Sample 21]

E-mail

件名: Delay in Shipment
差出人: "Hideo Kondo"<kondoh@kobeden.co.jp>
日付: 201-年5月25日1:35 p.m.
宛先: "David Anderson"<davida@pch.com>

Dear Ms. Anderson:

Thank you for your Order No. 106 for 400 units of PC-FV/66 printers.
I regret to say that it may be difficult to dispatch the goods within the time agreed upon.

As you know, the growing demand for personal computers has caused a world-wide shortage of ICs. The supply of the parts by our subcontracting manufacturers may be delayed two months, and that could affect our production schedule. I expect now that the full quantity could be shipped in early September.

I would suggest, therefore, that you take delivery of 200 units in July, and the other 200 units in September. I hope these split shipments will put you at less inconvenience. I await your direction.

Best regards,
Hideo Kondo

---

subcontracting manufacturers = firm being employed to do work as part of a larger project, usually supplying materials, labor, etc.

[Sample 22]

```
┌─────────────────────────────────────────────────────────┐
│ ○○○                    E-mail                           │
├─────────────────────────────────────────────────────────┤
```

To: "Takeshi Kawamura"<kawamura@naniwa.co.jp>
From: "Anil Mittal"<mittalan@manas.com>
Date: April 6, 201- 10:12 a.m.
Subject: Your Order No. 55 shipped.

Dear Mr. Kawamura,

We shipped your Order No. 55 of 300 units of reclining chairs, Model RD23-Y, by M/S Bengal, which left Mumbai yesterday, April 5, and is scheduled to arrive in Kobe on May 10.

The copies of the shipping documents were sent to you separately. We have drawn a sight draft on your bank for the invoice amount under the L/C No. L-5436. Please honor the draft when it is presented to you.

We hope you will find the quality satisfactory, and we look forward to receiving additional orders from you soon.

Sincerely,

Anil Mittal

    M/S = motor ship (a type of ship), M/V = motor vessel (p. 74)
    honor = accept or pay (a bill or check) when due

Exercise

🎧 13

Exercise A 次の会話を聞いて空所に適当な語句を補充し、それぞれの役割で会話の練習をしなさい。

A : Mr. Tanaka? Have you received our sample?

B : Yes, we finally received it yesterday.

A : Sorry _____ so long. When do you think you will test our sample?

B : I will check our R & D Lab's schedule about _____ they can start testing.

A : Could you test and qualify our sample as soon as possible?

B : Yes, we will do our best to finish the testing.

A : I'd be grateful if _____ let me know by e-mail or phone when you have completed it.

Exercise B 次の英文の日本語訳を書きなさい。

1. All of the goods you ordered in your September 5 e-mail are packed and ready for dispatch.

2. The order is so urgently needed that we would ask you to effect shipment by the middle of March if possible.

3. We regret that we are unable to dispatch in full your order for 2,000 dozen tea spoon sets as we have only 1,000 dozen of the goods in stock.

4. Your cargo of kitchen utensils reached Tokyo on October 12. Thank you for your prompt dispatch of our initial order.

5. We would ask you, therefore, to amend the credit, putting off the shipment time until the end of August.

Exercise C 空所の中の正しい語を一つ選びなさい。

1. (Attached / Accepted / Received) are the copies of the invoice and the bill of lading.

2. We (placed / dispatched / made) your Order No. S-350 by air freight on July 31.

3. Because of a material (rise / shortage / excess), we need at least five more weeks to complete production of the goods ordered.

4. This is the earliest vessel (useful / acceptable / available) now.

5. Could you (make / dispatch / take) the delivery a little bit sooner?

Exercise D 与えられた日本語の意味になるように空所に適切な語を記入しなさい。

1. ご注文は本日博多港を出港した玄海丸に積み込んだことをお知らせします。
   We are pleased to inform you that your order has been shipped today on M/V Genkai which (　　) Hakata today.

2. 積み荷が無事に到着し、ご満足いただけることを願っています。
   We hope that the shipments will arrive at your port in good condition and (　　) your complete satisfaction.

3. ご注文223の関係船積書類の写しを同封します。
   We are sending you the copies of the relative shipping (　　) of your Order No. 223.

4. ご注文の品は8月中に船積みします。
   We will ship the (　　) in your order during August.

5. ストが解決したらすぐにご連絡いたします。
   We will get in touch with you as soon as the strike is (　　).

Exercise E 与えられた日本語の意味になるように空所に適切な語を記入しなさい。

1. ご注文品を契約の期日までに船積できるように船積指図を送ってください。
   (shipping instructions)

2. 注文品が出荷され次第知らせていただけませんか。(our order)

3. 船荷証券は入手次第転送いたします。(Bill of Lading)

4. ご注文の品は11月の第一便にて発送いたします。(first vessel)

5. 追加注文をお待ちしています。

Exercise F 次の内容で英文Eメールまたは英文レターのメッセージを作成しなさい。

【状況】
① 有田製ティーカップセットの注文に関する船積みと包装に関する指図書が届いた。
② 商品は本日博多港を出た平成丸に積んだのでニューヨーク着は10月27日ごろの予定。
③ 関係船積み書類の写しを同封する。オリジナル書類は手形とともに銀行経由で転送する。
④ 商品が無事に届き、再注文をもらえることを願っている。

<BE一口メモ>

貿易取引の定型的条件（インコタームズ2010）

貿易取引では、契約の基本条件を定めた定型的取引条件が用いられます。これをこれは国際的な商慣習を基に出来上がったトレードタームズと呼ばれるものですが、トレードタームズにはいろんな種類があり、それぞれの内容や、解釈をまとめた国際的ルールがあります。そのうち最も多く利用されているものは国際商業会議所（ICC）が定めたインコタームズと呼ばれるものです。

積み地条件
- ① Ex Works (EXW) 工場渡し
- ② Free Carrier (FCA) 運送人渡し
- ③ FAS (FAS) 船側渡し
- ④ FOB (FOB) 本船渡し
- ⑤ C & F (CFR) 運賃込み渡し
- ⑥ CIF (CIF) 運賃保険料込み渡し
- ⑦ Carriage Paid to (CPT) 運送手配済み
- ⑧ Carriage and Insurance Paid to (CIP) 運送保険手配済み

揚げ地条件
- ⑨ Delivered at Terminal (DAT) ターミナル持込渡し
- ⑩ Delivered at Place (DAP) 仕向地持込渡し
- ⑪ Delivered, Duty Paid (DDP) 仕向け地持込渡し、関税込み

Chapter 13　決済の英語

[Sample 23]

Dear Bob:

Thank you for sending me the copies of the B/L and the Invoice for Order No. 125 by fax.

I am writing to inform you that I have arranged to remit $2,335 in payment for the invoice amount through our Osaka Chuo Bank to your account at the indicated bank. It may take 2 or 3 days until this remittance is posted by your bank.

We received our goods today from the forwarder here, and we thank you for your promptness in carrying out our order.
Regards,
Takuya

[Sample 24]

Dear Mr. Chung:

According to our records, we have not received your payment of $31,520 for your Order No. 22. Please note that this payment is five weeks overdue.

As you have always paid your bills punctually so far, we are concerned. However, in fairness to our other customers, we are unable to permit any further delays in your payment.

Please pay your bill by TT remittance right now, or e-mail me to discuss this payment. I am waiting for your early response.

Best regards,
Kentaro Okada

[Sample 25]

BILL OF EXCHANGE

No. Y-2012k

For US$1,432,000.00   TOKYO , DECEMBER 16, 201--

At THIRTY DAYS AFTER *sight of this FIRST Bill of Exchange (SECOND being unpaid)*
pay to _____ *or order the sum of* US DOLLARS ONE MILLION FOUR HUNDRED THIRTY TWO THOUSAND ONLY
Value received and charge the same to account of PUDONG SYSTEMS CO., LTD.
Drawn under SHANGHAI CENTRAL BANK, SHANGHAI
L/C No. CN123456 dated OCTOBER 3, 201--
To SHANGHAI CENTRAL BANK, SHANGHAI
　　2014 LUIJIAZUI RING RD. 200120
　　SHANGHAI, CHINA

TOKYO BUSSAN CO., LTD.
Signed
EXPORT MANAGER

収入印紙

Exercises

Exercise A 次の会話を聞いて空所に適当な語句を補充し、それぞれの役割で会話の練習をしなさい。

A: I'm glad to know that you're satisfied with our quality. Are you now considering _____ an order with us?

B: The quality is satisfactory. But what would your best price be, based on 1,000 kilograms per shipment?

A: Our price would be $2.00 per kilogram, Freight Prepaid, to your plant in Los Angeles, California.

B: Well, that seems a little high. Can you _____ it a little?

A: $2.00 is our best price, but we can offer you a 4-cent discount if you pay within 10 days after the invoice date, instead of 30 days. Is that acceptable to you?

B: Yes. That's _____. I'll send you our Purchase Order by e-mail later today.

A: Great. Thank you very much. I will wait for your Purchase Order.

Exercise B 次の英文の日本語訳を書きなさい。

1. We would appreciate your approving quarterly terms for our remittance instead of an L/C settlement.

2. Today, we remitted $126,750 to your account at the First Bank of California, Torrance.

3. Failure to pay on time will affect your credit rating. Please pay your bill in full by December 20.

4. If we do not resolve this matter by November 15, we may have to resort to legal means for collection.

5. We strongly recommend that you settle your outstanding payment within 10 days, so we may continue the good relationship we have had for many years.

Exercise C 空所の中の正しい語を一つ選びなさい。

1. We wish to call your attention to the enclosed account, which is now nearly six months (overdue / overlook / overstock).

2. We are enclosing a check for $30 in (placement / remittance / payment) for the samples.

3. This e-mail is to (inform / confirm / reply) you that your payment bill is three months' overdue.

4. Today I have received your Invoice No.15 by fax and found that the total (offered / invoiced / delivered) amount is $12,260, instead of $12,180. Please check the quantity and the amount in our order of June 14.

5. Thank you for your remittance on the (overdue / completing / outstanding) Invoice Nos. H-22 and H-23.

Exercise D 与えられた日本語の意味になるように空所に適切な語を記入しなさい。

1. 船積書類受領後全額支払われるべきことをご了解ください。
   Please note that payment should be made in (   ) after receipt of the shipping documents.

2. 航空便で送っていただいた商品の代金として300ドルの小切手を同封いたします。
   Enclosed is a check for $300 (   ) payment for the article you sent us by air.

3. 貴社の優れた信用状態を守り、強化するために支払いは10日以内にしていただかなければなりません。
   Payment should be made within 10 days to (   ) and further enhance your excellent credit standing.

4. 今日現在、貴社の取引銀行から振込み通知票は届いていません。
   However, we have not received the relative (   ) advice from your bank so far.

5. 支払い期日をお忘れになっていたかもしれませんが、今はもう送金を完了されているものと存じます。
   We presume that the (　　) date of your payment has slipped your mind, and that by now you have completed remittance.

Exercise E 次の文を英文に直しなさい。

1. 合計金額をお知らせいただき次第送金いたします。(remit/send)

2. 当方の記録によると、貴社からの支払い通知票がまだ届いていないようです。(payment notice)

3. 一覧後30日払いのD/A手形による支払いをお認め頂けませんか。(30 d/s)

4. 本日バークレイ銀行台北支店の貴社口座宛に55,800ドルを電信送金の手続きを完了しました。(your account)

5. 支払いは、商品受領後1週間以内に確実に電信送金いたします。(TT remittance)

Exercise F Chapter 11の信用状（Sample 20）の内容に基づいて次の為替手形を作成しなさい。

BILL OF EXCHANGE

No. _____
For _____   _____, _____

At _____ sight of this FIRST Bill of Exchange (SECOND being unpaid) pay to _____ or order the sum of

Value received and charge the same to account of _____
Drawn under _____
L/C No. _____ dated _____
To _____
    _____
    _____

収入印紙

Chapter 14　クレームの英語

[Sample 26]

E-mail

Subject: Wrong shipment of Order No. 1150
From:　　"Mike Hilling"<mike@calconp.com>
Date:　　April 12, 201- 4:28 p.m.
To:　　　"Ken Kinoshita"<kinoken@sgc.com>

Dear Mr. Kinoshita:

We received our Order No. 1150 of Portable Hard Disks yesterday. Thank you for your punctual shipment.

Upon checking the content, however, we found, as the Survey Report attached, that the quantity delivered and expressed in the invoice was different from what we ordered. The original quantity ordered on July 15 was:
　　　RHD-200G　800
　　　RHD-100G　200

The actual quantity received was:
　　　RHD-200G　200
　　　RHD-100G　800

As you can see, RHD-200G is short by 600 units and RHD-100G is over by 600 units.

We presume that this was due to clerical mistake at some stage ahead of packing. Anyway the large quantity difference may cause us over stock and confuse our original sales plan.

Please ship the additional 600 units of RHD-200G promptly. Shall we return the 600 units of RHD-100G at your expense? Or we would consider taking delivery of the whole quantity if you reduce the invoice amount by 3% to adjust for our inconvenience. Let us know which alternative you prefer.

I am awaiting your direction by e-mail.

Sincerely yours,

Mike

[Sample 27]

```
○ ○ ○                          E-mail
From:    "Saburo Suzuki"<Suzuki@totra.co.jp>
To:      "Nancy Brown"<nancyb@universaltoy.com>
Date:    May 10, 201- 3:18 a.m.
Subject: A matter of your May 8 under consideration
```

Dear Ms. Brown:

Thank you for your frankness in your e-mail of May 8, saying that you stated you are not perfectly satisfied with our instant noodle products.

We are surprised to learn from your e-mail that the quality of our products delivered was far inferior to the samples we sent last time. We have long experience in this line, and thanks to excellent quality control, the products have a good reputation. However, if you have the problems with our products that you indicated, we will try to do our best to improve them.

I would ask you to send me the Survey Report issued by a certified institution. We will get back to you on your claim after we review the report.

Best regards,

Saburo Suzuki

Exercises

Exercise A 次の会話を聞いて空所に適当な語句を補充し、それぞれの役割で会話の練習をしなさい。

A: Hello, how can I help you?

B: This sweater I _____ last week is not only uncomfortable, but it also has defected on the back.

A: I'd be happy to issue you a full refund.

B: But what about the rash it _____? I've been scratching all week.

A: I understand the situation and I'm sorry. How about I issue you an additional store credit for $20 to make up for the inconvenience?

B: That would make me feel a _____.

A: I'd be happy to do that for you and again my apologies for your inconvenience.

Exercise B 次の英文の日本語訳を書きなさい。

1. Nearly a month has passed, and we have heard nothing from you about the shipment.

2. Upon checking the supplied goods, we found there is a discrepancy between the goods sent and those invoiced.

3. We will file a claim with you for the losses we incurred.

4. Unless you take immediate action to correct this problem, we will be forced to end our services.

5. We hope you will understand that these circumstances are beyond our control.

Exercise C 空所の中の正しい語を一つ選びなさい。

1. On opening the contents, I found there were only 298 dozen DVDs, (though / but / however) we ordered 300 dozen.

2. Two of the total number of machine tools we bought (by / from / with) you do not work properly.

3. Thank you for your e-mail of August 10, calling our attention to the (wrong / punctual / prompt) shipment.

4. As you failed to make the shipment by the time agreed upon, we have no choice but to (place / pass / cancel) the order.

5. We have investigated closely and found that the shipment was wrong due to a (critical / clerical / crucial) error in our shipping department.

Exercise D 与えられた日本語の意味になるように空所に適切な語を記入しなさい。

1. この手違いは全く当方の過失であり、ご迷惑をおかけしていることに対してお詫び申し上げます。
   This mistake is entirely our own, and we apologize for the (　　) it is causing you.

2. 積み荷は3週間遅れて到着しましたが、それに対して何の説明もいただいておりません。
   The shipments have just arrived (　　) a delay of three weeks, and no explanation has been given us yet.

3. 早急に代わりの品を送っていただければ幸いです。
   We would be glad if you would send us a (　　) as soon as possible.

4. この種の誤りの再発防止のために最善をつくします。
   We will do our best to (　　) a repetition of this sort of error.

5. 商品は1週間以内に出荷するとの約束でしたが、長期の遅延により相当の迷惑を被っております。
   The goods were promised to be shipped within a week, and we have been (　　) to considerable inconvenience because of the long delay.

Exercise E 与えられた日本語の意味になるように空所に適切な語を記入しなさい。

1. 船積遅延が長期におよんでいることに失望しております。(delay)

2. 届いた品物の品質は見本とはちがっています。(we found)

3. 残念ながら届いた30箱のうち1箱は損傷を受けていました。(damaged)

4. これは重大な契約違反だと考えます。(breach of contract)

5. この問題は当方の事務的な手違いによって生じたものとの結論に至りました。(clerical error)

Exercise F 次の内容で英文Eメールまたは英文レターのメッセージを作成しなさい。

【状況】
① ご注文の博多人形50個のうち2個が壊れていたとのメールをいただいた。
② 当方の包装不良のためと判断した。
③ 取り換え品2個は本日航空便で送った。
④ 再発防止に努めたい。
⑤ 今後ともご用命をいただきたい。

<BEー口メモ>

数量に関する表現

　ビジネス取引においては、数字を抜きにしては考えられません。商品の質を評価するのも、数量を決めたり、取り引き値段を交渉したり、納期を決めたり、また業績や景気を判断する場合、営業活動の成否を評価したり、報告する場合などすべて数字が用いられます。したがって数字にかかわる英語表現があいまいであったり、誤っていると、自社や関係者に大きな迷惑や、損失をもたらすことになります。数字に関する基本的な英語表現をおぼえることはビジネスコミュニケーションの重要なツールと言えるでしょう。

50以上	50 units **or more**/not less than 50 units
50以下	50 units **or fewer**/not more than 50 units/not exceed 15%
5（年）以内に	**in** coming 5 years
30（日）以内	**within** 30 days
1,000を超える	**more than/exceeding/over** $1,000
120（ドル）未満	**less than**/below $120
5個で1ドル/15億ドルで	5 pcs. **for** $1/ ABC Corp. bought XYZ Inc. for $1.5 billion.
総計8,000ドルになる	Maintenance alone **amounts to** a total of $8,000.
20日付（の手紙）	letter **of** June 20 / offer of June 20/
10（日）以前	...effective **on or before** April 10/prior to April 10
10（日）以後	**on or after** April 10/start working from April 10
6日までに	subject to your reply received **by** May 6
15日まで	The offer is open **till** August 15
注文量300ダース	order **for** 300 dozen/order covering 100 tons of .....
注文額〜$150,000	Our order for 40 units of equipment **is worth** $150,000.
単価〜1ダース$34.5	We offer you this model **at** $34.50 **per** dozen. Prices are $230 for MK22 and $260 for MK23.
455ドル（価格）に値下げ	to lower the price **to** $455
価格は$300〜$400	Our DVD players cost **between** $300 **and** $400... cost as much as $400
$145の値がついた	personal computer **costing** $145
（維持費が）$850かかる	It will cost you $280 **a** year. / cost up to $1500 The maintenance will cost you $850 **a year**.
額面〜$12,000の手形	draft **for** $12,000 / LC **for** $23,540
手形期限一覧後30日	**at** 30 d/s
積期9月積み	**for** September shipment
定価から5%の割引率	5% **off** the list price / We will give you a five percent discount.

〜の値引き	10% discount **off** the list price/
（商品）番号〜	**Model No.** 234 / Sample No. TTS-55X/ RX332/Invoice HF220
約〜	**about** 300 metric tons / **approximately** 500 long tons
〜番に電話	call me at 882-3632/contact me **at** 882-3632
最長〜年まで	Leases for copiers are available **for up to** seven years.
年商10,000,000ドル	annual **sales of** $10,000,000
第2四半期	the **second** quarter
250億円の赤字	are ¥25 billion **in the red**
年2回の	**bi**annual / **semi**annual
週2回の（〜の刊行物）	**semi**weekly / **bi**weekly
隔週の	**bi**weekly / **semi**weekly
10%伸びる	Our sales for the fiscal 2010 increased by 10%.
年間生産高は10万トン	The annual output is 100 thousand tons.
海外売り上げが50%以上	Over 50% of our sales comes from the overseas market.
過去最高の売上げを達成	ABC & Co. has reached a record high of 1 billion yen annual sales.
営業は9時から5時まで	Our office is open from 9:00 a.m. to 5:00 p.m.
500万円の損失を出した	The company posted a loss of five million yen last year.
ゼロ	The growth rate was almost zero (nil) in 2010.
2倍以上の売上高	more than twice sales
20%上昇した	The cost increased by 20%.
2012年会計年度	fiscal year 2012 / FY2012
1960年に創業した	We started business in 1960 with capitalization of ¥10 million.
前年比10%伸びた	The sales for this year increased by 10 percent compared with the previous year.
3月末に失効する	This contract will expire on March 31, 2013.
1億円に及ぶ	The company spent an expense amounting to ¥100 million on R & D during these five years.
年率10%で	Our sales have increased at annual growth rate of 10 percent.
ビジネスウィーク誌の4月3日号に	The news appeared in the April 3 issue of Business Week. / ~in the Business Week for April 3.
営業日は月曜から金曜まで	We are open (from) Monday through Friday.

Cheat Sheet 1

Plain Word Glossary

簡潔でreadableな英語にするためには,長く、難解な語（heavy words）,複数の語からなる句（wordy phrases）、重複語（redundant words）, 陳腐な表現（clichés）などを避けて、できるだけ短い語（simple words）、なじみのある語(familiar words)を用いることです。

大げさ (pompous)	望ましい (better)
anticipate	expect
characteristic	trait
complete	fill out
fundamental	basic
furnish	give, send
regulation	rule
abundance	enough, plenty, a lot (or say how many)
acknowledge	thank you for
advantageous	useful, helpful
aggregate	total
alternative	choice, other
apparent	clear, plain, obvious
appropriate	proper, right, suitable
approximately	about
authorize	allow, let
comprise	be made up of, include
concerning	about, on
currently	now
endeavor	try
exclusively	only
finalize	end, complete
immediately	at once, now, soon
insufficient	not enough
marginal	small, slight
numerous	many (or say how many)
outstanding	unpaid
previous	earlier, before, last
reimburse	repay, pay back
requirements	needs
subsequently	later
substantial	large, great, a lot of
virtually	almost (or edit out)

冗長 (wordy)	望ましい (better)
as a consequence of	because
at an earliest convenience	soon
at all times	always
be in a position to	can
despite the fact that	although
for the sum of	for
from time to time	occasionally
in as much as	since
in due course	soon
in the near future	soon
it is necessary that	must
in the amount of	for
in reference to	about
owing to the fact that	because, since
prior to	before
provided that	if
with reference to	about

重複 (redundant)	望ましい (better)
absolutely perfect	perfect
actual experience	experience
advance planning	planning
advance reservations	reservations
advance warning	warning
all meet together	all meet
at 12 midnight	at midnight
at 12 noon	at noon
autobiography of my life	autobiography
awkward predicament	predicament
basic fundamentals	fundamentals
cease and desist	cease
cheap price	cheap
close proximity	proximity
cold temperature	cold
commute back and forth	commute
consensus of opinion	consensus
each and every	each
eliminate altogether	eliminate
end result	result
final outcome	outcome
for the purpose of	for
free gift	gift
green recycling	recycling
many wide-ranging ways	many ways
null and void	void
past experience	experience
personal opinion	opinion
pre-recorded	recorded
reason is because	reason is
regular routine	routine
regular monthly meetings	monthly meetings
revert back	revert
special discount	discount
unexpected surprise	surprise
whether or not	whether

二重否定 (double negative)	望ましい (better)
does not have	lacks
not certain	uncertain
not often	rarely
not many	few
not the same	different
not unlike	similar, alike
not...unless	only if
not....until	only when

陳腐 (clichés/jargon)	望ましい (better)
bread-and-butter issue	practical
Enclosed please find.....	We enclose....
few and far between	very few
in lieu of	instead of
in my opinion	*omit*
It is within our power...	We can...
last but not least	finally, last
needless to say	*omit*
pursuant to your request...	as requested
under the circumstances	*omit*

Cheat Sheet 2

和製カタカナ英語

　日本語の中には多くのカタカナ語が使われます。これは一見英語のように見えますが、英語本来の言い方ではないものも多いので、英語の文書や英語の会話でそのまま使うと相手に通じないことがあります。日ごろから正しい英語のつづりと意味を覚えておく必要があります。逆に考えると、普段使い慣れている和製カタカナ英語の正しい綴り、発音、意味を確認して覚えることによって英語の語彙を増やすことができます。

日本語	英語
アポイント	appointment
アルバイト	part-time job
アンケート	questionnaire
アンバランス	imbalance
インフラ	infrastructure
オートバイ	motorcycle / motorbike
オートロック	self-locking (door)
ケースバイケース	It depends.
ゴーサイン	green light
コストダウン	cost reduction
コンセント	outlet
サイン	signature/autograph
スマート	slim
タイムリミット	deadline
チラシ	advertising literature/ flyer
テーブルスピーチ	(make a) speech
テーマ	theme
デフレ	deflation
電子レンジ	microwave oven
プレート番号	license number
ネック（になる）	obstruction
ノルマ	quota
バイキング	buffet-style restaurant
バーゲン	sale
バージョンアップ	upgrade

日本語	英語
パンフレット	brochure / leaflet
フリーサイズ	adjustable / flexible / One Size Fits All
プラスドライバー	Philips head screwdriver
ベスト3	top 3
マイナスドライバー	flat head screwdriver
マスコミ	mass media
マンツーマン	one-on-one / man to man
マンション	condominium / apartment
メーカー	manufacturer
モーニングコール	wake-up call
ブランド品	name brands
プリント(資料)	handout/copy
フリーダイアル	toll free number
ラベル	sticker
リストラ	reengineering
リフォーム	remodel
コンクール	contest/ competition
コンパ	party
ベッドタウン	commuter town
シルバーシート	priority seat / seats for senior citizens
クラシック	classical
ロールパン	bread roll
ガソリンスタンド	gas station
キッチンペーパー	paper towel
フライパン	pan
エステ	beauty salon
アタッシュケース	attaché case（アタシェケース）
リラクゼーション	relaxation（リラクセーション）
エクシビジョン	exhibition（エクシビション）
イメージアップ	improve one's image
イメージダウン	hurt one's image
ネームバリュー	name recognition
（ホテルの）フロント	reception desk
マンネリ化する	become stereotyped
デメリット	disadvantage
フレッシュマン	new employee
ポリ袋／ビニール袋	polyethylene bag / plastic bag

Cheat Sheet 3

貿易取引に関する専門用語

　どの業界でもそうであるように、貿易取引においては取引に関して多くの専門用語が用いられます。国際的な取引はほとんど英語で行われることが多いので、その専門用語（technical terms）も英語が用いられます。これらを普通の言葉で表したり、説明したりすると逆に誤解を生じることになります。したがって貿易取引においては以下のような共通の用語を覚えて使用することが誤解なくスムーズなコミュニケーションを図ることができるといえます。

略語	用語	意味
	abandonment	委付
	advance payment	前払い
	advising bank	通知銀行
	agency agreement	代理店契約
NACCS	Air-NACCS	航空貨物電子通関システム
	All Risks	全危険担保
	amendment	（信用状の）内容訂正
	applicant	（信用状の）発行依頼人
	arbitration clauses	仲裁条項
	bank reference	銀行照会先
	beneficiary	受益者
	berth terms	個品運送契約
	blank endorsement	白地裏書
	breakage	破損
	Designated Hozei Area	指定保税地域
BAF	bunker adjustment factor	燃料高騰時割増し課徴金
	carton	段ボール箱
	charter party	用船契約
	commodity rate	品目別基本料金（海上運賃）
	consignee	荷受人
	consolidator	混載業者
CFS	container freight station	コンテナフレートステーション
CY	container yard	コンテナヤード
CFR	Cost and Freight	運賃込み条件
CIF	Cost, Insurance and Freight	運賃保険料込み条件

略 語	用 語	意 味
	credit inquiry	信用調査（信用照会）
	credit line	与信の限度
CAF	currency adjustment factor	平価変動時割増し課徴金
	customs broker	通関業者
	customs clearance	通関手続き
	customs house	税関
	deferred payment	後払い
	delivery	引き渡し、納期
DD	demand draft	送金小切手
	demurrage	滞船料
	description	（商品）明細
	destination	仕向け地
	discrepancy	ディスクレ、不一致
	dispatch money	早出し料
	distributorship	販売権
D/A	documents against acceptance	引受け書類渡し
D/P	documents against payment	支払い書類渡し
	drawee	（手形の）名宛て人
	drawer	手形振出人
	due date	満期（期限）
	duplicate sample	控え見本
	endorsement	裏書き
ETA	Estimated Time of Arrival	到着予定日
ETD	Estimated Time of Departure	出発予定日
	exclusive distributor	一手販売店
	exclusive selling agent	一手販売代理店
	firm offer	回答期限付きオファー
	Force Majeure	不可抗力
	forward exchange contract	先物為替予約
FPA	Free from Particular Average	分損不担保
	freight forwarder	通関・海貨業者
	freight payable (collect)	運賃後払い
	freight prepaid	運賃前払い
	General Average	共同海損
	governing law	準拠法
	IATA	国際航空運送協会
	import quota	輸入割当て

略語	用語	意味
	Incoterms	トレードタームズの解釈に関する国際統一規則
ICC	International Chamber of Commerce	国際商業会議所
JETRO		日本貿易振興会
LCL	LCL cargo	小口コンテナ貨物
	limit price	指し値
	liner	定期船
	litigation	訴訟
	mediation	斡旋・調停
	more or less terms	過不足容認条件
	negotiable	流通(譲渡)性のある
	negotiating bank	買取り銀行
	negotiation	手形買取り
	net weight	正味重量
	netting	相殺決済
	Notify Party(Also Notify)	着荷通知先
	OEM	相手ブランドによる製造
	on board notation	船積み注記
	order	指図(指図人)
	original	原本
	partial shipment	分割積み
	port of call	寄港地
	principal to agent	本人対代理人
	shipper	荷送人
	shipping advice	出荷案内
	shipping documents	船積み書類
	shipping mark	荷印
	shipping sample	船積み(先発)見本
	shipping space	船腹
	shortage	着荷不足
	SR & CC	ストライキ、暴動内乱危険
TT	Telegraphic Transfer	電信送金
TTS	telegraphic transfer selling (rate)	電信売り相場
	terms and conditions	取引条件
	transshipment	積み替え
	vanning	コンテナ詰め
WA	With Average	分損担保

Cheat Sheet 4

部課の名称および役職名

会社の部課名や役職名はそれぞれの会社の組織内容によって異なりますし、同じ役職名でもその権限や責任は会社や国によって異なることがあります。実際のビジネスにおいては自分や相手の権限を確認し合いながらコミュニケーションを図ることが大事だと言えるでしょう。

役職名		部署名	
最高経営責任者	Chief Executive Officer(CEO)	営業	Sales
最高財務責任者	Chief Financial Officer(CFO)	運輸	Transport
最高執行責任者	Chief Operating Officer (COO)	海外営業	Overseas Sales
執行役員	corporate officer	海外事業	Overseas Operation
名誉会長	Honorary Chairman	企画	Planning
会長／理事長	Chairman / Chairperson	品質管理	Quality Assurance/ Quality Control
社長	President		
代表取締役	Executive Managing Director/ Representative Director	苦情処理	Customer Relations
		警備	Security
副社長	Executive Vice President	経理	Accounting
専務取締役	Senior Managing Director	研究開発	Research and Development
常務取締役	Managing Director		
重役／取締役	Director/Member of the Board	工場	Plant
社外(非常勤)役員	Outsider Director	厚生	Welfare
社長室長	Manager, office of the president	購買／資材	Purchasing/ Procurement
理事	Director		
経理担当役員	Comptroller/Controller	広報	Public Relations
非常勤役員	Outsider Director	労務	Labor Relations
顧問	Executive Advisor	財務	Finance
相談役	Advisor	出荷	Shipping
監査役	Auditor	流通	Logistics
社長付	Assistant (Attached) to President	人材開発	Human Resource Development
秘書	Secretary/Corporate Secretary	人事	Personnel
支配人	General Manager	人事管理	Human Resource Development
本部長	Division Director	技術	
部長	General Manager / Department Manager	生産技術	Production Engineering
事業部長	Business Division (General)	設計	Design
支店長	Branch Manager	宣伝	Advertising

役職名		部署名	
海外出張所長	Liaison Office Director	倉庫	Storage
所長	Division Manager	総務	Administration/General Affairs
副事業部長	Deputy General Manager		
営業所長	Sales Office Manager	特許	Patent
室長／部付	Manager (of a section)/Officer Manager	秘書室	Secretariat
		業務	Operation
課長補佐／代理	Deputy (section) Manager	情報処理	Data Processing
次長	Deputy Department Manager	文書	Documentation
係長	Assistant (Section) Manager	法務	Legal
主任	Supervisor	保全／保守	Maintenance
取締役会	Board of Directors	マーケティング	Marketing
次長	Deputy General Manager		
部長待遇...	with general manager status	輸出	Export
室長	Chief / Director / Head of a section (division/department)	輸入	Import
		営業推進部	Sales (Business) Promotion Department
課長	Manager / (section chief)		
参事	Associate Director (chief) (of a section)		
		調達課	Procurement Section/Division
副参事	Deputy Associate Director (Chief of a section)		
		製造部	Manufacturing Department
主幹	Senior Manager		
主事	Manager	資材部	Procurement Department
主査	Assistant Section Chief		
課長代理	Acting Section Manager	調査部	Information & Research Division / Inquiry Section (Department)
係長(主任)	Chief Clerk / (section chief)		
社員(部員)	staff (member)		
営業部長	Chief of the Sales Department / Business (sales) Manager	宣伝部	Advertising Department
工場長	Factory Manager / Plant Superintendent / Plant Manager	企画部(室)	Planning Department (office)
		販売促進部	Sales Promotion Department
PR担当	Communications Manager		
経理担当	Treasurer	企画開発部	Project Planning & Development Department
班長	Team Leader		
秘書(幹事)	Secretary		
支店長	General Manager / Branch Manager	秘書室	Secretary Section (Secretariat)
参与	Counselor / Consultant	社長室	Office of the President

Cheat Sheet 5

アメリカ英語とイギリス英語

　日本ではアメリカ英語に慣れている人が多いかもしれませんが、同じ英語でもアメリカとイギリスではかなり違う面があります。語彙そのもののちがいは割と知られていますが、そのほかにも、綴り、文法、語法(表現)にも違いがありますし、また発音やイントネーションにも違いがみられます。non-native である日本人はどちらの英語を用いてもかまわないという考え方もありますが、アメリカ英語、イギリス英語のどちらであるかが分かっていれば、可能な範囲で相手(reader)にわかりやすい英語を書くように心がけるのがいいと思います。

アメリカ英語	イギリス英語	意味
store	shop	店
zip code	postcode	郵便番号
stove	oven	オーブン
cell phone	mobile phone	携帯電話
zero, oh	nil	ゼロ
schedule	timetable	予定表
reservation	booking	予約
package	parcel	小包
liquor	spirits	アルコール飲料
résumé	CV (curriculum vitae)	履歴書
paper towel	kitchen paper	キッチンペーパー
national holiday	bank holiday	祭日
vacation	holiday	休暇
two weeks	fortnight	2週間
parking lot	car park	駐車場
driver's license	driving licence	運転免許証
airplane	aeroplane	飛行機
round-trip ticket	return ticket	往復切符
bill	note	紙幣
call	ring	電話する
bill	check	請求書
trash, garbage	dust, litter, rubbish	ごみ
advertisement	advert	広告
drugstore / pharmacy	chemist	薬局
apartment	flat	
expiration	expiny	満期

アメリカ英語	イギリス英語	意味
Officer / CEO Chief Executive	Managing Director / MD	最高経営責任者
automobile / car	motor car	自動車
sidewalk	pavement	歩道
mailbox	postbox / pillar box	郵便ポスト
crosswalk	pedestrian crossing	横断歩道
railroad	railway	鉄道
line	queue	待ち行列
salesclerk	shop assistant	店員
to go / takeout	takeaway	持ち帰り用料理
canned food	tinned food	缶詰
flashlight	torch	懐中電灯
downtown	city centre	市街地
mail	post	投函する
store	shop	店
subway	underground/tube	地下鉄
learned	learnt	learnの過去形
spilled	spilt	spillの過去形
esthetic	aesthtic	美的な
practice	practise	練習する
repair	mend	修理する
catalog	catalogue	カタログ
analog	analogue	アナログ
program	programme	プログラム
tire	tyre	タイヤ
jewelry	jewellery	宝石
check	cheque	小切手
disk	disc	ディスク
analyze	analyse	分析する
civilization	civilisation	文明
apologize	apologise	わびる
realize	realise	悟る
color	colour	色
humor	humour	ユーモア
favorite	favourite	お気に入りの
harbor	harbour	港
counterclockwise	anti-clockwise	反時計回り
canceled	cancelled	cancelの過去形

アメリカ英語	イギリス英語	意味
canceling	cancelling	取り消すこと
inquiry	enquiry	照会
ton	tone	トン(重量単位)
traveler	traveller	旅行者
fulfill	fulfil	満たす
judgment	judgement	判断
aging	ageing	ageの現在分詞形
story	storey	階
license	licence	免許
Monday through Friday	Monday to Friday/ Monday till Friday	月曜から金曜まで
in the future	in future	将来
on the weekend	at the weekend	週末に
two thousand nine	two thousand and nine	2009
What's up? / Hi!	Alright? / Alright mate?	元気ですか
O.K.	All right	大丈夫
very much	indeed	大いに
want, like	fancy	好む
maybe	perhaps	たぶん
be busy	be engaged	(電話が)話し中
hang up	ring off	電話を切る
nice, great	brilliant	すばらしい
Could you...?	Would you mind...?	…していただけませんか
See you.	Cheers.	じゃあね
Go get pizza.	Go to buy pizza.	ピザを買ってきて
He is a good player.	He is a good player.	…が上手です
—Yes, absolutely.	—Yes, he is, indeed.	ほんとにそうですね
Do you have the time?	Have you got the time?	お時間ありますか
I wanna try...	I want to try...	…してみたい
I'm gonna leave...	I am going to leave...	もう帰ります
I got to go.	I have to go.	行かなくっちゃ
You are welcome.	My pleasure./Not at all.	どういたしまして
either [íːðə(r)]	either [áiðə]	いずれかの
advertisement (advertisement / -tize- [ædvərtáizmənt]/[-̩təz-]	advertisement [ədváːtismənt]	広告
schedule [skédʒuːl]	schedule [ʃédjuːl]	予定

Cheat Sheet 6

複合語

複合語には複数の単語をただ並べて用いるものと、それらをハイフンでつないで、形の面でも一語のような使い方をするものがあります。複合語を用いると単語の節約になるので、新聞、雑誌などでは名詞だけでなく、名詞、動詞、副詞、形容詞、前置詞など様々な品詞の語を組み合わせて新しい複合語が造られる傾向があります。

no-cost	金のかからない	give your daughter a no-cost party
high-definition	高品位の	high-definition television
high-resolution	高解像度の	high-resolution TV camera
easy-to-follow	わかりやすい	easy-to-follow instructions
straight-up	本当の、信用できる	Here's the straight-up story.
on-the-job	現場での/ 実践での(教育)	on-the-job training/ on-the-job writing/on-the-job learning/ on-the job education
in-chief	担当責任者	editor-in-chief (…in-the-chief)
up-front	前もっての	up-front (advance) payment 前払い pay ~ up front 前金で払う
in-house	社内(組織内)の/自社製	in-house newsletter/ in-house translator/ in-house tool
in-depth	完全な、徹底的な(副詞から形容詞化した)	The online version, available only to FORTUNE subscribers, offers the most in-depth information about America's leading businesses.
wait-and-see	成り行き次第の	wait-and-see attitude
sought-after	需要の多い(人気のある)	Writing is one of the most sought-after attributes in the business world today.
forward-looking	前向きの、進歩的な (cf. backward-looking)	Most of forward-looking managers always write in plain English.
deep-rooted	根深い	deep-rooted problem
well-established	しっかりした	We are looking for a well-established agent.
well-known	有名な	We are one of the well-known manufacturers of optical instruments.

clear-cut	明確な	The link between alcohol and crime is clear-cut.
long-running	長期にわたる	long-running campaign
end-of-month	月末の	We are sending you our end-of-month statement.
computer aided	コンピュータを使った	Computer-aided design (CAD) is the use of computer technology for the design of objects, real or virtual.
self-absorbed	自分のことしか頭にない、自己陶酔の	Avoid self-absorbed statement.
time-honored	昔からの、ゆいしょある	The changing business cards is a time-honored tradition both in America and Japan.
lift-off	近代化への乗り出し	China's military lift-off has caused some diplomatic problems.
first-ever	初めての、史上初の	University of Leicester produces the first-ever 'world map of happiness.'
time-consuming	時間のかかる	This effort may become extremely time-consuming.
error-free	誤りのない	a straightforward, error-free, no-gimmicks sentence
crystal-clear	明晰な(=clear)	It is crystal-clear that….
eye-glazing	〔退屈で〕目もかすむほどの、生気のない	eye-glazing copy
toll-free	受信人払いの	Use toll-free numbers for ordering.
user-friendly	使いやすい	user-friendly computer
disabled-accessible	身障者が利用できる	disabled-accessible toilet
face-to-face	直接会っての	Let's discuss any issues at face-to-face meeting.
hand-to-mouth	その日暮しの	hand-to-mouth living
step-by-step	段階的な/一歩ずつ進んでいく	step-by-step approach/ step-by-step increase/ step-by-step instructions
state-of-the-art	最新の	state-of-the-art DVD player
wall-to-wall	びっしりの(一面に敷き詰めた)	wall-to-wall copy
word-of-mouth	口コミの、口伝への	Since we rely on referrals and word-of-mouth advertising, this is essential for success.

year-on-year	Year-on-year changes とは前年同期（月、四半期など）と比べた変化のことである	Year-on-year changes are changes in levels expressed over the corresponding period of the previous year.
top-of-the-line	最高の	He spent money on buying top-of-the-line wood rather than machinery.
like-for-like sales	既存店ベースの(同じもの同士を比較する)の売上げ	Using like-for-like sales is a method of valuation that attempts to exclude any effects of expansion, acquisition, or other events that artificially enlarge the company's sales.
mind-numbing	まったく退屈な	mind-numbing copy
epoch-making	画期的な	This may lead an epoch-making business.
cost-performance	コストと性能(機能)のバランス/支出した費用に対する満足度の割合	Cost Performance of Automobile Engine Plants
grass-roots	草の根運動、民衆に根ざした、根本的な	grass-roots campaign /～democracy
mass-market	大(量)市場	mass market/ mass-production (distribution)
name-brand	有名ブランド(品)を安く手に入れる(name brand とハイフンなしでも使う)	get name-brand for less/ name-brand goods/ name-brand item
one-stop	一度ですべて用が足せる	one-stop shopping /one-stop guide
three-week	3週間の	Try out the product in your office for a free three-week trial.
year-end	年末の	year-end sales campaign
home-care	在宅の	Home care, (commonly referred to as domiciliary care), is health care or supportive care provided in the patient's home by healthcare professionals.
non-English	英語を母語としない	non-English readers
non-profit	利益を目的としない	NPO
non-government	政府ではない	NGO
co-hosted	共催イベント	first-ever co-hosted event

Cheat Sheet 7

主要な貿易関係書類

　貿易取引においては、専門用語と同様に、多くの書類（documents）が用いられます。昔はそれらの多種類の書類をいちいちtypewriterを用いて手作業で作成していたので貿易実務はそれだけで難しいものだと考えられてきました。しかし最近では貿易文書の簡易化とコンピュータ化すなわち貿易取引の電子化が進んだおかげで、貿易取引のスピードアップがはかられるようになりました。

Air Waybill		航空貨物運送状
Application for Amendment to L/C		L/C変更依頼書
Application for Credit		信用状開設依頼書
Application for Negotiation		手形買取依頼書
Application for Opening L/C		信用状開設依頼書
Arrival Notice		貨物到着通知書
Arrival Notice		書類到着通知書
Average Bond		共同海損盟約書
Bill Bought		買取り手形
Bill for Collection	B/C	取立て手形
Bill of Exchange		為替手形
Bill of Lading	B/L	船荷証券
Booking Note(Memo)		船腹予約申込書
Captain's Protest		海難報告書
Cargo Application to		保険申込状
Cargo Boat Note		カーゴ・ボート・ノート
Certificate and List of Measurement and /or Weight		重量容積証明書
Certificate of Insurance		保険承認書（証明書）
Certificate of Origin: Form A		原産地証明書:様式A
Claim Note		損害求償状（船会社）
Claim Note		損害求償状（保険会社）
Clean B/L		無故障船荷証券
Combined B/L		複合輸送用船荷証券
Combined Transport B/L		複合運送船荷証券
Commercial Invoice		(商業)送り状
Confirmed L/C		確認信用状
Consular Invoice		領事送り状

Container Load Plan	C.L.P.	コンテナ内積付表
Crate		クレート梱包
Credit Note		貸記票（振り込み票）
Customs Invoice		税関送状
Customs Procedure Entry System	CuPES	通関手続き申請システム
Debit Note		借記票（引落とし票）
Delivery Order	D/O	荷渡し指図書
Demand Draft		要求払い手形
Dishonored Bill		不渡り手形
Dock Receipt	D/R	輸出貨物引取証
Documentary Bill		荷為替手形
Documentary L/C		荷為替信用状
Exchange Contract Slip		為替予約票
Export Calculation Sheet		輸出採算表
Export Declaration		輸出申告書
Export License	E/L	輸出承認証
Export Permit		輸出許可書
Health Certificate		衛生証明書
House Air Waybill		混載業者発行のAWB
House Bill of Lading		混載業者発行のB/L
Import Declaration	I/D	輸入申告書
Import License	I/L	輸入承認証
Import Permit		輸入許可書
Inspection Certificate		検査証明書
Insurance Policy		保険証券
Invoice		送り状
Irrevocable L/C		取消不能信用状
Letter of Guarantee		貨物引取り保証状
Letter of Credit	L/C	信用状
Letter of Guarantee	L/G	保証状
Letter of Indemnity	L/I	補償状
Mate's Receipt		本船受取証
Master Air Waybill		航空会社発行のAWB
Master Bill of Lading		船会社発行のB/L
Notice of Damage		予備クレーム
Notice of Readiness		荷役準備完了通知書
Open Policy		予定保険証券

Order B/L		指図式船荷証券
Order Sheet		注文書
Packing List		包装明細書
Price List		価格表
Proforma Invoice		見積り(仮)送り状
Provisional Insurance Application		予定保険申込書
Purchase Note		買約書
Quotation		見積書
Received B/L		受け取り船荷証券
Release Order		引渡し指図書
Sales Confirmation		販売確認書
Sales Contract		売買契約書
Sales Note		売約書
Sea Waybill		海上運送状
Shipped(On board) B/L		船積み船荷証券
Shipping Advice		船積み通知書
Shipping Instructions		船積み依頼書
Shipping Order		船積指図書
Sight Bill		一覧払い手形
Specifications		仕様書
Stale B/L		時期経過船荷証券
Stand-by Credit		融資保証信用状
Straight B/L		記名式船荷証券
Survey Report		鑑定報告書
Tally Sheet		検数票
Through B/L		通し船荷証券
Trust Receipt	T/R	貨物担保保管証
Usance Bill		期限付き手形

TEXT PRODUCTION STAFF

edited by   編集
Mitsugu Shishido   宍戸 貢

cover design by   表紙デザイン
Ruben Frosali   ルーベン・フロサリ

CD PRODUCTION STAFF

recorded by   吹き込み者
Josh Keller (AmE)   ジョシュ・ケラー（アメリカ英語）
Deirdre Merrel-Ikeda (AmE)   ディアドリー・イケダ（アメリカ英語）

Eメール時代のグローバルビジネス英語
Global Business English for E-mails and Letters

2010年 3月30日　初版発行
2015年10月20日　第4刷発行

著者　福田　靖
発行者　佐野 英一郎
発行所　株式会社 成 美 堂
　　　　〒101-0052東京都千代田区神田小川町3-22
　　　　TEL 03-3291-2261　　FAX 03-3293-5490
　　　　https://www.seibido.co.jp

印刷・製本　倉敷印刷株式会社

ISBN 978-4-7919-6482-6　　　　　　　　　　Printed in Japan

・落丁・乱丁本はお取り替えします。
・本書の無断複写は、著作権上の例外を除き著作権侵害となります。